The
Walrus's Handbook

**Understanding ourselves — a continuum from the
biological to the emotional, social and spiritual aspects**

From an original illustration by Sir John Tenniel 1820-1914

'The time has come', the Walrus said,
'To talk of many things.'

'Through the Looking Glass', Lewis Carroll

The
Walrus's Handbook

Understanding ourselves — a continuum from the biological to the emotional, social and spiritual aspects

Hazel Skelsey Guest

First published in Great Britain by
Archive Publishing
Dorset, England

Designed at Archive Publishing by Ian Thorp

© 2016 Archive Publishing
Text © Hazel Skelsey Guest, 2016

Hazel Skelsey Guest asserts the moral right to be
identified as the author of this work

A CIP Record for this book is available from
The British Cataloguing in Publication data office

ISBN 978-1-906289-29-4 (Paperback)

The illustrations inside the book are reproduced by courtesy of the illustrator
Ian Thorp

www.archivepublishing.co.uk
www.transpersonalbooks.com

Printed and bound
at LightningSource

ACKNOWLEDGMENTS

The Appendix reproduces the paper *Maslow's Hierarchy of Needs: the Sixth Level* by Hazel Skelsey Guest, which was first published by the British Psychological Society in *The Psychologist*, December 2014, vol.27, no.12, pages 982-983.

Part 2, *Step By Step*, reproduces some of the material in the paper *The Scale of Responses: emotions and mood in context*, by Hazel Guest and Ian Marshall, which was published in the *International Journal of Psychotherapy*, 1997, vol.2, no.2, pages 149-169.

CONTENTS

PART 2: STEP BY STEP

PART 3: CONCLUSION

ADDENDA

CHARTS AND DIAGRAMS

PART 1: NEEDS MUST

PART 2: STEP BY STEP

APPENDIX

PREFACE

As the Walrus said, 'the time has come'. I have reached an age which is termed 'elderly' and the time has come to write down those matters which have been important to me during my lifetime. In some respects the time is long past as much has been forgotten, but certain matters still stand out clammering to be expressed. Hence this book.

As these pages are partly about motivation it is fitting that they should start with my own motives in writing them, which are several. The first is to demonstrate that our physical, emotional, social and spiritual aspects are inter-related in a seamless continuum, the result of our biological evolution.

The second is to present two psychological theories and to show that both are complete. Part 1 deals with motivation theory, the psychology of those inner forces which persuade or impel us to act, and Part 2 presents a system for understanding our reactions, how and why we respond to situations in the way we do. These two theories have been tried and tested by me, both in my practice as a psychotherapist and in my own daily life, and I have found them to be revealing and comprehensive.

The third aim is to publish a book which is of use to counsellors and psychotherapists of all orientations, as well as being of interest to the general public.

Finally I aim to be accurate, concise and to the point, which is the reason why this work is relatively short in keeping with its title as a handbook.

Part 1, Needs Must, is about motives. For as long as literature has existed there have been those who have manifested a curiosity about the psyche of individuals, a desire to understand the inner world of thoughts and desires, the forces that drive us sometimes unreasonably to our own destruction. Books and plays have explored these themes, whether they be tragic or comic, and those that reveal insight have survived the test of time. One has only to cite the Bard. Where would *Othello* be without its deceit and jealousy, *Macbeth* the lure of power, the *Merchant of Venice* a sense of justice, or *Hamlet* the procrastination which resulted from a struggle between doubt and moral outrage?

During the twentieth century psychologists developed a number of different motivation theories and 'Needs Must' is based on that one which is arguably the most widely known. It has certainly stood the test of time and has been applied in the world of business management as a guide to motivating employees.

The central theme is Abraham Maslow's[1] renowned theory, the Hierarchy of Needs[2] including his 1967 addition[3]. Over the years I have found that this system works and is comprehensive as it includes all possible motivations other than survival itself. To correct this particular omission survival has been added to the bottom of the Motivation Hierarchy (diagram 1).

The reader will find repeated references to this diagram throughout the pages of Part 1, and a comprehensive account of how Maslow's 1967 list of needs evolved from his better known 1943 version will be found in the Appendix.

He based his theory on the assumption that we are the products of biological evolution and that those needs which motivate us are embedded in our genes. So the first chapter traces those motivations through the evolution of species. Each of the seven levels is described in a chapter of its own, followed by 'Pre-potency' which explains why they are arranged in a specific order, and 'Childhood' which reveals the same hierarchical order in our early development.

The remaining chapters which are arranged in no particular order other than how they occurred to me, examine familiar motives and where they might be located within the hierarchy.

Part 2, Step By Step, presents the Scale of Responses which deals with our moods, how we respond to situations, and how quickly those moods can change. This theory is the work of Ian Ninian Marshall[4], a Jungian psychiatrist, who developed the Scale in 1969 as part of a therapeutic system which he called 'Sequential Analysis'[5]. He died in March 2012 and never published this system which, as his former pupil I find regrettable. All that has been published so far is an academic paper describing the Scale which appeared in 1997[6] and it is on this that Part 2 is based.

Step By Step is all about how people respond to situations according to their mood and how those responses can change, sometimes quite rapidly. Since communication involves at least two people interacting each of whom has his or her own characteristics, the situation can become quite complicated.

Frequently we find people responding to us in ways we did not expect because we failed to take into account, or even to observe, their frame of mind. Television serial sitcoms thrive on such situations since they provide unexpected twists and turns to the plot which keep the audience watching for episode after episode.

Part 2 ends with several imagined scenarios for the reader to try out the information so far gleaned, with suggested analyses in the penultimate chapter.

Parts 1 and 2 are in contrast. Maslow was eminent in his profession, Marshall less so. The 1943 version of the Hierarchy of Needs[7] rapidly became well-known across the industrialised world because of its application to motivation in the workplace. By contrast The Scale of Responses never took off because the original academic paper was published at a time when this was not a hot topic professionally. This is a great pity as I believe it contains wisdom and has much potential for improving relationships.

It happens frequently that academic papers are overlooked simply because they are buried amongst a proliferation of other material and the right people do not have their attention drawn in that direction. Both Marshall's Scale and Maslow's 1967 addition to his Hierarchy, suffered similar fates. This is one reason for publishing both of them now in book form.

What these two systems share in common is their wide applicability. In my practice as a transpersonal psychotherapist, I used both systems often and usually with success. Clients found them easy to understand and apply, giving rise to a number of therapeutic insights.

Of course I am not recommending them as a do-it-yourself tool to relieve deep-seated psychological ills, but rather as a means of understanding ourselves and others so as to be able to make our ways through life more happily, with more success, and with fewer mistakes and regrets. Any deeper exploration of our own psyches should be undertaken with the guidance of a qualified counsellor or psychotherapist.

Any psychological topic needs to be illustrated with examples from life, and this is certainly true in both parts of this book. This presents an author with a problem. Because of a requirement for confidentiality it is necessary to obtain permission from those people whose experiences are being described, and then their identities have to be disguised by altering one or two details such as names, where they live, and so on.

Because of the expected difficulty of tracing the whereabouts of former acquaintances and the fact that their stories would have to be partially fictionalized anyway, the solution was to use a mix of my own experiences and made-up examples. Hopefully this will not detract from their illustrative value.

In giving examples I have included my own views on their analysis. These are merely opinions and should be treated as such. They are not set in stone and this is not an exact science. Whenever disagreement arises it is suggested that the reader write down his or her views and keep that note with the book.

It might be said that some of the examples are simplistic, lacking the sophistication and complications from side issues that life so readily throws at us. But that was intentional. As a former teacher I am well aware that clarity is essential when introducing a topic. First present the bare bones and then assemble the whole skeleton. It is only when this has been accomplished that it is time to think about dressing it up. Similarly when teaching the laws of motion it is customary to start by ignoring complications like friction, air resistance and energy loss due to heat production on impact. These can all be included at a later stage.

Finally, as its title proclaims this is a handbook, a manual. The chapters are short and to the point to facilitate its use for reference. I hope these pages will prove to be both informative and useful.

Cambridge
United Kingdom
19th September 2015

PART 1:

NEEDS MUST

DIAGRAM 1

The Motivation Hierarchy

Maslow's Hierarchy of Needs, 1967 version, has six levels from
Physiological to Intrinsic Values.
In addition a seventh level, Survival, has been included at the bottom.
The reader may wish to copy this diagram onto a loose sheet
for easy reference.

CHAPTER 1

The Evolution of Needs

Let us suppose that you plan to camp in some wild remote region with a view to getting back to nature for a few days. What provisions would be considered necessary for such a venture? Presumably food, water and shelter would come to mind as priorities. If the environment will not provide these then they will need to be taken with you. They are the basics for sustaining life.

It would also be advisable to consider any possible dangers from the wild life. If the area has grizzly bears then a gun might be a good idea, or mosquitoes then a net. It would also be wise to take a first aid kit to protect against infection — that is unless you have sufficient knowledge of natural remedies to be able to rely on the local flora.

These basic needs can be summarised under the headings physiological and safety which are common to us all. But these two needs do not end here. We lock our doors at night in order to feel safe from burglars. Those who flee from bombs and bullets seek safety in a refugee camp where aid agencies strive to provide them with food, water and shelter, as well as protection from disease by the provision of sanitation and medical supplies. We try to get on with our neighbours in order to avoid creating enemies who might harm us, and we insure our property in case it is destroyed in some calamity.

However these basic drives alone, although they sustain and preserve us and are necessary for our well-being, cannot be regarded as sufficient for human life. We have all sorts of other needs. A child needs love and support, an elderly person living alone needs company, counselling groups keep reminding us of the need for self-esteem, and we all need to achieve some degree of success in whatever we try to accomplish. And this is not all. From time to time we need to have our spirits uplifted, which may be achieved via music, religion, communing with nature, the ardent pursuit of some worthwhile cause, or in a myriad of other ways.

Where do these complex needs come from? They are potential drives in all of us regardless of whether or not our lives have allowed their satisfaction to manifest in practice, and so it can be argued that they are all biologically based. They are in our genes and our behaviour reflects the attempt to satisfy whichever of these drives happens to be to the fore. They are hard-wired into us and must therefore be the product of evolution.

In recent years we have been treated to many fascinating TV documentaries about animals, often revealing behaviour which was previously unknown. We have learned that chimpanzees obtain food by using tools to crack nuts and to extract insects from crevices. We have seen mother leopards teaching their cubs the skills they will need as adults, and meerkats sharing lookout and nursery duties. Birds construct nests ready for the eggs that will be laid, and the intricacies of a spider's web have caused us to marvel. We have been awed by the distances travelled during migrations, whether it be groups of birds, butterflies or whales.

If it is said that these behaviours are instinctive, is this a way of dismissing them by comparison with us humans on the assumption that we do things consciously having made a decision to act?

Such behaviours are always for a purpose. Hunting is to provide food. Nest-building is to provide a suitable and safe support for eggs and young chicks. Digging a burrow is intended to offer a safe haven from predators. Migration finds the best environments for feeding and breeding according to the seasons. So what we used to dismiss as mere instinctive behaviour is actually adaptation to satisfy needs, primarily for food and safety and to produce and rear young, which in turn procure survival of the species.

On tracing through the evolutionary tree from the earliest single-cell life forms to creatures like whales and dolphins as well as the primates and ourselves, it is clear that needs have evolved. The most basic of drives is to *survive* (diagram 1) and primitive single-cell organisms did this by taking in nutrients and by reproduction, although how they went about satisfying these *physiological* imperatives varied.

It is not being suggested here that primitive organisms had a will to survive and therefore sought to find food and to reproduce. That would be unacceptably anthropomorphic. Rather it is the other way round. Those earliest life-forms which happened to survive were those that took in nutrients and subdivided, that is they fed and reproduced and

therefore their genes survived. In time, as evolution progressed, survival of the individual and of its genes became the driving force while food
and reproduction became the means by which that goal was achieved.

Going up the evolutionary tree we come to fishes. Today's fishes
have an awareness of danger from predators and the need to escape.
Reptiles also are aware of the need for *safety* (diagram 1), and they seek
hiding places or have developed hard shells and weapons with which
to defend themselves. They take the trouble to lay their eggs in a safe
environment even if no further interest is taken in the young, like the
turtle which struggles up a beach to bury her eggs in safety and then
abandons the hatchlings to fend for themselves. This is not maternal
care as we understand it but at least it is a beginning.

We now know that mother crocodiles shelter their young inside
their large mouths, whereas not so long ago it was mistakenly thought
that they were eating their offspring!

Next on the evolutionary tree we come to birds and mammals.
These creatures invest a great deal of time and energy in rearing their
young, and to this end many mammalian species find it advantageous
to bond together in co-operative groups. In birds the grouping instinct
is most noticeable during migration, but it should be remembered that
pairing is also a form of bonding. Some species of bird pair for life
while others just for the rearing of one family.

With mammals co-operation is the norm with but few exceptions.
When threatened, elephants shelter their calves in the middle of the
group of formidable adults. Meerkats share the duties of rearing the
young and take it in turns to act as lookout when the rest of the group
forage for food. Lions and wolves hunt co-operatively in packs. This
instinctive togetherness can be called the need to *belong*, which is the
next rung up from *safety* in diagram 1.

Our domesticated pet dogs have inherited the wolf's pack instincts,
with recent research showing how distressed they become when left
alone for any length of time. The owner is seen as pack leader whose
absence is devastating. Contrast pet cats who are loners like their
larger cousins the tigers, leopards and cheetahs, seeming to bond with
their territory rather than with others of their kind. Lions are the feline
exception.

Bonding also gives rise to the concept of 'us and them'. To protect
their territory most mammalian groups will fight tooth and claw against
an invading group of the same species. Many of us were shocked on

seeing our first TV documentary which showed apparently lovable chimpanzees setting out to patrol their territorial boundary with the express intention of killing members of a rival group. Battles existed in the animal world long before the first humans appeared.

On a different evolutionary branch insects such as ants, bees and termites have catered for their survival and safety needs by developing their own brands of social cohesion. In these communities it appears to be the group's survival which is all important, not the individual's. It may be this characteristic which makes insects seem so alien, since we humans set much store by our own individuality and self-worth.

On the other hand spiders appear not to have evolved an instinct for belonging at all. In fact there is a species of spider in which the female is much larger than the male and she eats him after mating. One marvels at the strength of his instinctive motivation to mate by approaching her at all.

Comparison between fishes and insects leads to some speculation. The evolutionary branches which led to these two groups, separated a very long time ago. Did this occur before or after the development of the instincts for *safety* of the individual and to *belong*? Did certain insects dispense with the need for individual safety as their need for protection and defence of the group took precedence? Insects seem to have developed their belonging instinct separately from other branches of the evolutionary tree, thus accounting for their distinctively different group behaviour.

The need for bonding and togetherness, the ability to distinguish between 'us and them', requires a form of communication. We humans rely on voice, gesture and facial expression but these are by no means the only viable methods.

Bees certainly use gesture to communicate where sources of pollen are to be found, but insects in general use chemicals, in other words the sense of smell. In fact smell is a sense which is important for many species, both on land and in the sea. Many mammals communicate by scent-marking. It is only in us humans that this sense has deteriorated, presumably through lack of use.

Another method of communication is by colour change, as in the chameleon. We also communicate when we blush, but because this is involuntary the message conveyed is not necessarily what we would wish.

Parrots are a puzzle. They have evolved with the ability to vocalise and yet they appear to use this skill only to copy humans and other creatures, not as a means of communicating with each other. They are intelligent so perhaps they will eventually develop a vocalised language.

No two individuals are exactly the same, so it is inevitable that groups which co-operate and work together will require leadership to keep them functioning, thus producing alpha males and females. A herd of elephants is led by a matriarch, a group of gorillas has its silver-back, and a pack of wolves has its alpha couple who alone are allowed to mate and reproduce.

In some species there is not only a leader but also a hierarchy of status amongst the members of the troop together with a jockeying for position by bettering oneself. Chimp females vie to become the alpha male's favourite as this makes the winner alpha female. Thus arises the idea that some individuals are more capable or stronger or more important than others, and it is no joke being the one who is at the bottom of the list. This is motivation for *esteem*.

When modern humans eventually came onto the scene what exactly did they add to this list of needs which govern behaviour? Living within extended family groups there would have emerged a recognition of individual talents such as successful hunting or the ability to produce a perfect flint, and there would have been leaders and followers.

Ethologists studying examples of ancient cave and rock art tend to link these paintings with religious beliefs and magical rites. But could not at least some of them have been simply the result of exuberant self-expression by an individual whose ability to draw was admired?

Eventually groups expanded in size with the discovery of agriculture and therefore the ability to settle in one place. This enabled specialization of occupation, so individuals were able to develop particular skills and enjoy rewards for their expertise. Instead of small communities of hunter-gatherers we now had settlements consisting of farmers, potters, metal-workers, builders as well as rulers and administrators. In those societies in which specialization was encouraged the need to *self-actualize* — to fulfil one's potential — gained impetus. Individuals aspired to improve their lot by using and developing whatever talents they possessed.

With expanding populations come internal conflicts, so there arose a need for more formal control with conventions of right and wrong behaviour. In fact this may not be exclusively a human development since we observe amongst other species — for example apes — that certain behaviours are considered acceptable and others are not. Be that as it may, at the dawn of civilization humans prescribed laws along with agreed conventions of right and wrong behaviour to preserve social cohesion, and the invention of writing enabled those laws to be recorded for future reference. Control by government and edict had been born.

This stage also involved the rise of organized religions with a priestly class. Unable to explain the forces of nature, superstition and fear abounded. So leaders were able to reinforce their power by claiming that they were divinely inspired and that their edicts came from the gods. This meant that no-one could dispute them, and in fact the idea of the divine right of kings lasted well into our current era.

Now that populations could be organised along with the opportunity for specialization of tasks according to aptitude there emerged a leisured class. This encouraged appreciation of the arts and philosophy and enabled at least some of the populace to become literate. The civilizations of ancient Egypt, Greece and China are probably the best known examples of cultures which have left a lasting legacy.

Alongside came a sense that some qualities have value in themselves, such as beauty, usefulness, harmony, justice, wisdom. One might then be motivated to put one's energy into creating beautiful objects, arguing for mercy, promoting virtue, or pursuing knowledge and truth. Motivation by *intrinsic values* had arrived.

Thus the complexity of all motivating drives evolved by the simple process of finding a behaviour to satisfy a particular need, and then that behaviour in turn became a need to be satisfied, and so on. The fundamental starting point was the relationship between survival on the one hand and food and reproduction on the other.

The forces which motivate each one of us arise from inborn needs which are encoded in our genes as the result of biological evolution. But we are not the only intelligent and advanced species. Is it possible that dolphins have a conscience, a sense of values? Or have they evolved some other drive unknown to us? We have no way of knowing, so I shall stay with what we do know, namely those motivating urges which we humans are all capable of experiencing because they have become biologically-rooted in our genes as the result of our evolutionary history.

The continuum of seven categories of motivation which we have inherited through our biological evolutionary development, and which are illustrated in the diagram of The Motivation Hierarchy, will form the basis for all succeeding chapters of Part 1: 'Needs Must'.

All levels except *intrinsic values* are to do with self-interest and this raises the question of how did a concept of self evolve? Plants take in water, nutrients and sunlight in proportion to their needs and they reproduce, so they have physiological needs which are in their own interests for survival. But having no brain they can have no sense of self. Animals which take action to avoid or escape from danger, have a sense of that which needs to be protected and to my mind that constitutes the spur for developing a sense of that entity we could call self.

A herring hides itself in a shoal of herring, not a shoal of pilchards. There is an instinct that draws it to its own kind. The eventual evolution of a sense of self identity has its origin in this instinct to belong, which in turn is a solution to the need for *safety*.

When we come to mammals we find some that not only have a sense of self but also cognition of self-image. Any species which hides its body from predators or which conceals itself when creeping up on its prey, has some sense of how it is perceived by others. This is self-image and goes further than a mere sense of self. Contrast the proverbial ostrich hiding its head in the sand in the mistaken belief that, because it cannot see therefore it cannot be seen. This is a step towards having a self-image but the bird is certainly not there yet.

Recent experiments with mirrors have revealed that elephants and dolphins recognise their own reflections and this has been hailed as proof that they have a sense of self. But for me this is evidence of much more. It shows not only that they have cognition of self-image but also the reasoning ability to work out that what they see in the mirror is not reality but a reflection of themselves.

CHAPTER 2

The Motivation Hierarchy

It is possible that part of diagram 1 may already seem familiar to you. It has been around for decades, has become popular in training courses for managers of organizations and businesses worldwide, and has been reproduced in countless psychology books and articles written both for the popular market and for students and academics. It is one of the standard theories for psychologists studying motivation.

The section from *physiological* to *self-actualization* has become so well known as the Hierarchy of Needs that I felt a different name was required for the expanded version which is reproduced here. Hence the name 'Motivation Hierarchy' for the latter.

The Hierarchy of Needs first appeared in 1943 in a paper[1] written by the American psychologist Abraham Maslow[2]. His aim was to devise a theory of human motivation by defining those needs which are common to us all.

Previously he had carried out research into the behaviour of captive monkeys. The days had not yet arrived when film crews could be sent out for several months into the wild to record animals in their natural surroundings, and anyway so little was known about animal behaviour at that time that working with captive animals was at least a start.

In carrying out this research Maslow was struck by the many similarities between monkeys' needs and those of humans. This suggested to him that they were driven by similar motives. In particular he was deeply impressed on observing that infant monkeys, when deprived of the comfort and reassurance of their mothers, would cuddle anything soft and warm such as a soft toy or a fur blanket.

The similarities led him to the idea that there are certain basic motivational needs in humans that are rooted in our evolutionary biology. By definition these drives must potentially be common to all humans even though there exist individuals in whom not all are manifested in practice. After all, those who live at a subsistence level in a third world country are preoccupied with the planting of crops and praying for rain. They do not concern themselves with development of their talents and living life to the full even though, as humans, in another environment this might well be their preoccupation.

To avoid cultural differences he had to come up with a list of basic human needs of which each is capable of interpretation in a variety of ways. His solution was these five broad headings: *physiological, safety, belonging, esteem, self-actualization*, to which he added *intrinsic values* in 1967 shortly before his death[3]. In their diagrammatic representation they are read from bottom to top.

The extra level at the bottom, *Survival*, is an addition of my own. It seems obvious and perhaps Maslow just took it for granted. Anyway I cannot conceive that he would have raised any objection to its inclusion.

In view of the variety of human experience in terms of goals and desires, just seven categories may seem to be unduly limited. However, as these chapters will demonstrate, they are indeed all-encompassing provided each category is interpreted as broadly as possible.

Maslow's scheme was called the Hierarchy of Needs, the assumption being that motivation is the result of experiencing some need. Need is different from want or desire. A need is always for some purpose, a student needs to study in order to pass exams, a seamstress needs fabric and certain pieces of sewing equipment in order to make a garment. Similarly each of us needs to have these seven categories adequately satisfied in order to be as fit, healthy and fulfilled as is humanly possible, both in body and in mind.

Of course there are those in whom some of these needs are not satisfied for whatever reason, whether it be due to a genetic disorder, permanent physical injury, or living under demanding environmental or political conditions. Nevertheless these drives are in our genes whether or not they are realized in practice. They are our human inheritance and are potentially present in every one of us.

As Part 1 is all about the interpretation and application of the Motivation Hierarchy the reader is advised to make a loose-leaf copy of Diagram 1 for ease of reference.

CHAPTER 3

Survival

Survival is so clearly a motivation that it seems odd that Maslow left it out of his list which, in its final form, started with physiological needs and ended with intrinsic values. Perhaps he felt it was too obvious to require a mention.

Similarly on starting to write this book it did not occur to me at first that survival should be included, but in the course of composing the first chapter something struck home. I seemed to be arguing that, as each need evolved creatures sought satisfaction in ways that then became yet another need. So need A was satisfied by solution B, and B became a need which was satisfied by solution C, and so on. This implies that each originated as a means of satisfying some prepotent urge. Therefore there must be some basic requirement at the base of the hierarchy giving rise to all the others. So what is the drive that physiological solutions like food and reproduction satisfy? Obviously: survival.

Survival means the continuation of life, either that of the individual organism or that of the genes. In modern times the cult of the individual is so strong that we usually mean the former when considering humans. Nevertheless the motive to survive through our genes is still active even though we do not think of procreation in those terms. Hormones coursing through our bodies ensure the strength of the sex drive. We lavish care and love on our offspring with the intention that they shall enjoy what we ourselves lacked, and hope we can make up for our own mistakes vicariously through them. What is this if not, at least in part, a drive to survive through posterity?

When referring to animals it is the other way round. When we speak of the survival of tiger, panda or platypus we are concerned with the continued existence of the species and not of any one individual. In spite of all the work done by naturalists the majority of us still do not think of animals, not even the most intelligent, as 'persons' — except perhaps our own pets.

Survival is usually regarded as the strongest of all human motivations. A person who is drowning will find superhuman reserves of strength to fight to the surface. Some survivors of serious car accidents have reported that just before impact time seemed to slow down, enabling them to make split-second decisions which saved their lives. People have recovered from severe injuries or illnesses against all the odds apparently due to their will to survive. If starving one will eat anything to stay alive.

Unlike other creatures we are able to think in abstract and symbolic terms. So we might aim to survive in the products of our efforts or in others' memories. When enjoying a work of art, whether it be music, painting, literature, we may feel as if we are directly in touch with its creator. Shakspeare, Beethoven, Leonardo all live on in their masterpieces. Inventors live on in their creations, and pensioners in the autobiographies which they record for their grandchildren. The current interest in tracing one's ancestry is yet another way of bringing the past back to life.

Every one of the seven levels of motivation has its downside and survival is no exception. Survival's negative is death, which includes suicide. Consequently the will to survive can create a fear of death which inevitably must befall every one of us sooner or later. It is the prospect of oblivion, of just not existing any more, that scares, and is countered by the variety of religious beliefs about an after-life, whether they promise eternal bliss in Heaven, spirit communication, or reincarnation.

This fear of death has given rise to a belief in the sanctity of life — but only human life. We are quite prepared to kill animals for sport or for food but believe that human life must be preserved at all costs. Indeed this doctrine is at the heart of a doctor's Hippocratic Oath.

Now that the extinction of species is better understood there is a growing perception that all life is sacred, a view which has always been held by Buddhists.

All life-forms are interconnected in terms of the food chain, and ultimately our own survival is threatened by encroachment on habitats and over-harvesting. So it is surprising and potentially disastrous that respect for all life is not universal.

CHAPTER 4

Physiological Needs

Physiologically we are very similar to all other mammals. Our skeletons differ only in small details, so much so that vets and doctors use exactly the same names for the various bones of the body. Our organs, too, are similar although ruminants, such as cattle, have developed a different digestive system. We are so alike that medical research is carried out on rodents and monkeys to provide cures for human ailments. This means that at the physiological level our needs are the same as, or very similar to, those of all other mammals.

This level of motivation is basic and is all about the needs for food, water, warmth, exercise, rest, and anything else that keeps the body healthy such as medicine and surgery when sick or injured, as well as the satisfaction of the hormonal urge for sex.

Along with the survival instinct physiological needs first appeared at the dawn of evolution, well before any glimmer of consciousness began to arise. So we have inherited a system whereby many of our bodily functions do not require conscious control, albeit they may need regulation by the brain at an unconscious level.

The immune system tracks down foreign invaders and eliminates or expels them. The digestive system extracts nourishment from food. The lungs and heart take oxygen and pump it to every extremity. Levels of essential chemicals are monitored. The nervous system carries out instructions from the brain so that our muscles do what we want. Thus our physiological needs are cared for, to a large extent without any conscious intention or effort on our part.

If we become stressed the autonomic nervous system comes into play creating the fight-or-flight response. When tired we can relax and recover our strength and vitality during sleep. The brain which controls all of this, is regularly described as a miracle of organization with many levels of complexity beyond the most sophisticated computer.

This is a truly marvellous body and all we have to do is look after it. But it is so incredibly efficient at what it does that we tend to take its functions for granted and often indulge in practices which are potentially harmful. Many of us consume alcohol to excess, do not eat a healthy diet, or fail to take enough exercise, and sooner or later we suffer as a consequence.

The regular Friday and Saturday night booze-up in our towns and cities is not only injurious to the individual concerned, it is also undignified, gives our society a bad name, and frequently produces brawls which can turn nasty, even fatal. Why do we do it? Have we no respect for our own bodies and minds, let alone the welfare of others who get caught up in the fray?

We do not always go to the doctor when symptoms first appear, so they worsen, perhaps to the point of incurability. Our failure to seek help is in spite of the fact that modern medicine can cure so many different illnesses with drugs, it can repair arthritic joints and broken bones with surgery, and now is able even to operate on cataracts in the eye. Sometimes all that is required is a visit to an optician, dentist or physiotherapist to avoid a worsening of the problem, but we put it off.

Then there is the adrenaline-fuelled thrill of extreme sports or simply of driving a fast car. This may lead to taking risks which result in injury. The need is then for surgery, perhaps a long period of recuperation, and in extreme cases the patient's daily physiological needs have to be supplied by a team of carers.

Of course, in some cases it can be the body itself which lets us down. Fatal conditions can be inherited via the genes, a problem which modern research is beginning to tackle now that the human genome has been identified.

So far we have considered those needs which are life-preserving, but our own behaviour can actually generate the creation of new physiological needs which are destructive in their effect. These include the smoker's need for yet another cigarette, the alcoholic's need for a drink, and the drug addict's need for another fix. These conflict with the body's natural requirement for healthy abstinence, but addiction alters the body's chemistry to such an extent that the symptoms constitute a physiological drive which over-rides the natural ones and becomes a new all-consuming motive.

When choosing a means of satisfying a need we do not always opt for the best solution. We shall see that this applies to all levels in the Motivation Hierarchy, each of which has its negative and destructive aspects.

CHAPTER 5

Safety

This level of motivation is not just about safety from the threat of immediate danger — it is also about ensuring one's safety in the future, in other words security.

Anyone living a subsistence existence in a country that is subject to droughts, wants to ensure the food and water supply in whatever way possible, perhaps by digging deep wells for drinking and irrigation. Having large families is intended to ensure that there will be help in growing food and that parents will be looked after in their old age. Without such measures there is no sense of security in the future and instead the ever-threatening danger of destitution engenders fear.

Safety is about preserving oneself from the threat of harm, and in a modern capitalist society this can come in many forms, financial and social as well as physical. Doors and windows are closed at night to protect against the intrusion of burglars, and if these fail then we can call in the police in the hope that they will recover our stolen property. Insurance policies do not compensate for the loss of objects of sentimental value but they do offer the security of financial recompense so that the stolen articles can be replaced.

If about to travel to a country which has an endemic disease it is wise to have the appropriate injections beforehand as well as taking out health insurance.

We take simple precautions against pests — powders and sprays to keep ants and flies at bay, and local councils provide rubbish clearance to avoid disease and a plague of rats.

Barring an untimely fatal accident or illness we all have to grow old eventually. After retirement, although there are no longer the costs of commuting to work and of raising a family, other expenses tend to increase as our bodies wear out and require all sorts of extra treatment and aids not provided by the National Health Service. So young adults endeavour to ensure their financial future by buying their own homes and securing good pensions. However house prices in the UK have risen so high that many cannot afford the initial payment for a mortgage nor the premiums for a private pension to boost the minimal state pension, all giving rise to an increased sense of insecurity for the future. In fact growing numbers struggle to pay for food and heating right now.

The National Health Service looks after us when ill or injured, although it is creaking under the pressures of an ever-expanding and ageing population. Especially hard-pressed are Accident and Emergency departments, because the local doctors' appointment system means one gets seen sooner by going to hospital. The solution would seem to be to have local walk-in centres in every town centre. After all, when the NHS first came into being patients just turned up at the doctor's surgery and waited their turn. There was none of this having to wait until 8.30am the following day to arrange a time to attend for an appointment with a doctor one does not know, or waiting three weeks for an appointment with the doctor of one's choice.

To protect against serious infections we have vaccinations and quarantine. However the bugs look after their own safety needs by mutation to become immune to existing drugs. Our response is yet more research. This is a war with sometimes one side winning and sometimes the other.

We teach our children not to play with matches or sharp knives, but leave some safety issues to the state or our local council. Following devastating floods in some parts of the UK in recent years it was generally felt that better flood defences were needed to keep homes safe in the future. Traffic lights, pedestrian crossings and speed cameras are meant to protect us against road accidents, although these measures have proved to be insufficient. Roads and pavements need repair to avoid accidents, a law bans the keeping of certain dangerous breeds of dog, there are health and safety laws governing practices in places of employment and notices warn the public of natural hazards.

In fact health and safety is such a big issue that some argue the state has gone too far, not only by reducing peoples' personal sense of responsibility for ensuring their own well-being but also by introducing completely ridiculous regulations. One example was the banning of the game of conkers in school playgrounds to avoid the remote possibility of a child getting hurt. By contrast one wonders why rugby is still played when it is quite clearly a dangerous sport in which serious injuries are known to occur.

The downside to the need for safety includes irrational fears and paranoia. This is when the pursuit of security becomes an obsession. Take for example the person who puts so many locks and bolts on doors and windows that it can be compared to Fort Knox.

Common phobias such as fear of enclosed spaces, flying, heights, spiders, snakes and what have you, are all basically expressions of this same need for safety, however irrational, which is achieved by assiduously avoiding the feared situation.

On a national level there is our nuclear deterrent the existence of which is justified by some on the grounds that it protects us against a nuclear attack, but which is disputed by others. Arguments for and against are ongoing.

I can remember when our country was indeed in danger. World War Two broke out when I was ten years old. To preserve the safety of these islands we went to war, young men and women joined the forces, and my father who had fought in the trenches in France during the First World War, volunteered in the ARP (Air Raid Precautions) in addition to his normal employment in central London. During the blitz my brother, who was still a student and owned a motorbike, served as a dispatch rider for the ARP in his spare time.

We lived at the eastern edge of the capital and my father used to come home from work on the last train around midnight, sometimes pursued by enemy aircraft because sparks from the steam engine could be seen from the air in spite of the blackout.

With our neighbour next door they made a concrete underground shelter which spanned our two gardens, and both families slept there every night, females on mattresses on the floor, males on bunks above us.

My safety was further ensured by being evacuated for a while. I was one of the girls from my junior school who, together with half a dozen nuns to look after and educate us, were housed in Evelyn Waugh's home, Piers Court, in the village of Stinchcombe, Gloucestershire while he was away serving with the forces. But in fact I was back in London during both the blitz and the arrival of the V1's and V2's.

Like all other institutions schools had to introduce safety measures. The teachers and oldest girls at my secondary school were drafted into fire-watching duties at night, and the precautions taken to protect us from the V1's without too much interruption to our lessons were something of a pantomime. These weapons, dubbed doodlebugs, were slow and noisy so you could see them coming and you were quite safe until the engine cut out. Even then you could see the direction in which they would fall. So our school safety system when the air-raid siren sounded was for one teacher to stand on the front lawn facing the direction from which they came, while another stood by the controls to a loud electric bell. When teacher number one waved, teacher number two rang the bell and everyone poured out into the reinforced corridors. Thus was our safety ensured.

The V2 rockets were a totally different matter. From them there was no opportunity to secure one's safety. Their arrival was unannounced and devastating, creating fear. In an attempt to avoid panic when the first of these exploded the government gave out information that it was the result of a faulty gas main, but as more and more 'gas mains' went up the public saw through the propaganda and realised this was a new and deadly weapon.

In spite of all this my childhood confidence never wavered and I retained a conviction that we would remain safe.

There seems to be no end to wars. Today's civil conflicts and terrorist armies in the Middle East and North Africa have given rise to a crisis of vast numbers of refugees seeking safety in other countries, only to find that they are accommodated in inadequate camps by the host countries which cannot cope with their numbers. They have achieved safety from the bombs and bullets, and in some cases torture, only to end up faced with deprivations of another kind.

CHAPTER 6

Belonging

Belonging is the first and most fundamental of the social needs. Loneliness can be very distressing and is often one of the perils of growing old. We all need some kind of social network involving relationships, starting with family but spreading out to include friends, acquaintances, and organisations. This is also the need for love.

Hermits appear to be an exception since they deliberately choose to live a life of solitude. But there are not many true hermits and we know little about their states of mind. Maybe they have replaced the need for human company by communion with nature.

Psychologists affirm that the bond between mother and baby is essential for the future well-being of the child. Within families there is usually a strong sense of togetherness, involving loyalty and mutual assistance during times of adversity. We also form firm friendships outside the family, whether this be in the school playground or in the workplace or wherever. Even joining a street gang can be a way of satisfying this need as it confers on the individual a particular sense of identity associated with the group.

In fact identity is all about those groups to which we belong. One person would describe himself as male, in his forties, married, father of two, home-owner, a businessman, atheist, member of the local tennis club, likes to join his buddies in the pub for a drink. Another sees herself as female, single, in her twenties, teacher, flat-dweller, Anglican church-goer, likes to read whodunits. Linking ourselves to such groups is the way in which we define ourselves.

Social life has many levels of relationship. People join clubs, meet neighbours at church or while shopping. They do things together even though they may not know each other well. Part of the thrill of attending a football match or the last night of the Proms is the atmosphere of all those other folk sharing in the same spectacle and experience.

In this era of computer technology, the days of the regular get-together around a neighbour's piano or the pub's dart board are disappearing. Social networking on the internet seems to have taken over this role of providing contact with others. However it is one step removed from actual contact and is more like communication with a fantasy being. In my opinion it does not provide an adequate sense of relationship and belonging that is so necessary for a healthy social life, especially since individuals can hide behind a false identity.

Take alienation a stage further and we find individuals who lack this sense of belonging altogether, namely the homeless. They have left their families for whatever reason and are no longer members of society. Their need for belonging is satisfied only by association with each other or by having the companionship of a dog.

Most criminals have rejected society in favour of their own kind, and the Mafia, or Cosa Nostra, are close-knit on an exclusively family basis, bound together by loyalty as well as fear.

Immigration occurs now in such numbers that immigrants tend to associate within their own ethnic or national groups rather than integrating with the host nation. This can spawn ghettos in which the failure to integrate is perpetuated, creating the danger of future conflict between neighbouring groups as well as failure to identify with the nation as a whole. This last is a recipe for civil unrest on a national scale. In Britain the spirit of camaraderie which united us as a nation when confronted by a common enemy during World War Two, could be lost. The solution is to foster a sense of pride in belonging to the host nation before a state of social fragmentation is reached.

Of course nationalism can go too far. While singing patriotic songs during the last night of the Proms may be inspiring and harmless, the same cannot be said of Nazi gatherings during the late 1930's which served to emphasize the differences between those who belonged and those who did not.

National, racial and religious loyalties create differences which often escalate into conflict and can endure from generation to generation. Europe has a history of several centuries of conflict between Catholics and Protestants, the remnants of which are still alive in Northern Ireland. Many Muslims still identify with those past brethren who fought against the Crusaders. The current hatreds occasioned by Israel's takeover of most of Palestine are not going to go away.

The downside of this need to belong also includes jealousy and possessiveness as well as feelings of rejection and abandonment. It involves the 'us and them' syndrome, prejudice and aggression against those who do not belong to one's own group, those of another race or religion, foreigners in general, the elderly and disabled, fans of the other football team, or members of a neighbouring street gang.

There is no way of getting past this. Belonging automatically involves a definition of those who do not belong. The danger can be mitigated by enlarging one's group categories. For example identify with the human race rather than with one's nation. But that fails to take into account the fact that others still identify with their nation or ethnic group and can become aggressors.

Moreover the human race still has a bad record for its dealings with animals. Even those of us in the western world who have a bond with our pet dogs and cats, yet have no compunction about swatting a fly — except Buddhists, of course.

CHAPTER 7

Esteem

When at the motivational stage of esteem, what matters is a person's perception of where he or she stands in relation to the rest of the group. It has three aspects namely self-esteem, esteem in the eyes of others, and esteem for others. The need is for self-confidence, friends who will encourage, and role models who will inspire. Anyone who struggles to achieve requires support, and it helps if there is someone who has previously taken a similar route and can be a source of inspiration.

Today we see this need for heroes particularly in sports and pop music, but unfortunately the heroes themselves do not always live up to expectations. After all, they set out on their careers with their own ambitions in mind and not with a view to providing the public with role models.

When young our primary role models were parents and older siblings, and later perhaps teachers. We respected them, partly because they were bigger and stronger than us and also because we understood that they knew how to do things that were still beyond our own capabilities.

Then there are the heroes and heroines of fairy tales and adventure stories who uphold right against wrong, good against evil. Little girls want to be regarded as both good and beautiful, just like Cinderella or Snow White and not like the wicked witch. Little boys want to be brave and adventurous like Sinbad or Superman. The popularity of the Harry Potter stories is due to their archetypal portrayal of the struggle between good and evil with good triumphing in the end.

As for self-esteem, educationists are well aware that children need encouragement for their strengths rather than criticism for their weaknesses. A sound basis of self-confidence in childhood bodes well for success later on. Bullying is a deliberate attack on the sense of self- worth, and recent incidents that have been reported in the news reveal that consequences can be dire, sometimes resulting in the victims' suicide. The sad fact is that bullies are attempting to boost their own sense of self-esteem by putting others down.

Some seek to satisfy this need through fame. Many a teenage girl has dreams of becoming a famous fashion model, and boys of scoring goals as a star footballer. Olympic medal-winners must surely be gratified at the praise and admiration in which they are held by their fans.

However esteem does not have to be won at the expense of others nor in a blaze of glory. Someone who had a happy childhood with a sense of self-worth, may well grow up to live a contented but humble life, valued by those with whom that life is shared.

The need for esteem can be experienced collectively, as in national pride. It could be argued that the troubles in Northern Ireland were the result of wounded self-esteem within a section of the populace in the face of being governed by what they perceived as a foreign power. When once they were given their own parliament the mutual enmity between the Unionists and Republicans subsided to such an extent that Ian Paisley and Martin McGuinness actually became friends, frequently enjoying a joke in each other's company. After all, this degree of autonomy must have felt even better to both of them than being ruled either by Westminster or by Dublin.

In some countries certain groups are held in higher regard than others because of their birth. Britain has its class system though modern democratic values are bringing about changes. The class system based on family is being replaced by one based on wealth, but this latter no longer carries the respect which was formerly accorded to the well-born when people 'knew their place', when 'upstairs' and 'downstairs' were separated by well-defined rules of conduct.

There is much more social mobility now that theoretically anyone can go to university, whereas when I was young you had to have wealth or win a scholarship. However the huge debts with which graduates are now lumbered may return us to something approximating that earlier situation, with the less profitable of the new universities having to close down.

More deep-seated are the caste system in India and distinctions based on race. The slave trade of the 17th to 19th centuries still has repercussions today with those of African descent treated as inferior. Although South Africa's apartheid system was abolished, largely due to the charisma of Nelson Mandela, former attitudes have not been eliminated. In the USA discrimination against black people has become illegal, but they still struggle to be treated equally with whites, especially in relation to the operation of the law by predominantly white police. Even having a coloured President does not seem to have given the black population the reassurance that it craves.

In addition to discrimination and prejudice the downside to the need for esteem includes lack of ambition, low self-worth, embarrassment, self-deprecation, bullying, envy, disrespect, scorn and degradation. It is these characteristics which breed many of society's ills, such as the commission of crime and vulnerability to various forms of criminal exploitation such as being groomed for sex or for terrorism. This theme is enlarged upon in the chapter on Deficiency.

CHAPTER 8

Self-Actualization

The term self-actualization means living one's life to the full, realizing one's full potential. A person is able to develop whatever talents and pursue whatever interests come to the fore. Needless to say, in the whole of the human population there are relatively few people who reach this level of motivation and even fewer who actually satisfy this need in full.

This is the drive to be successful and to further one's own career. It is also the desire to earn as much money as possible in order to live a lifestyle of luxury in which all activities of choice are available. Consequently there is also the danger of becoming a workaholic, or of being a slave to greed and losing sight of one's other needs.

Here we find ambition, perseverance, striving to attain a dream, pursuit of the career of one's choice, while on the downside are people who are ruthless and so driven by ambition that they ride roughshod over others in order to achieve their goals.

In terms of relationships self-actualization is about finding the right partner, congenial friends, and bringing up one's children to be happy and successful. On a practical level it is about ensuring one's home provides comfort and serves the family's needs with furnishings suitable to one's tastes and lifestyle, and ensuring convenient travel arrangements. It is also about having hobbies and interests which delight and refresh, and the ability to indulge personal eccentricities. Inevitably all this entails the need to have enough money to be able to pursue these ends satisfactorily.

In terms of social mores self-actualization includes being able to express one's identity freely as a member of a minority, whether it be gay, coloured, disabled or whatever. It is only relatively recently that the UK parliament passed anti-discrimination laws which were intended to make the satisfaction of this need possible for everyone but it is clear that they have not yet been in place long enough to eliminate old prejudices.

The downside to self-actualization not only includes ruthlessness and greed but also failure, disappointment, overwork, too narrow a focus, and barriers to advancement. In Britain the days in which women were the property of their husbands are long gone. They gained the same voting rights as men in the early decades of the twentieth century and equal pay after World War Two. So theoretically they should now have the same opportunities as men to reach their full potential, but many career women still seem to experience a 'glass ceiling' in spite of the law against sexual discrimination.

However self-actualization does not necessarily have to involve ambition and career. It is possible for a labourer to feel fulfilled in his work and family life, or a housewife in raising her family. Presumably nuns and monks and missionaries feel fulfilled in their vocations.

People vary considerably in terms of what sort of life-style would give them satisfaction. For one it might involve a full social life with lots of friends and frequent parties. For another it could be a fruitful career in research, producing new theories or useful inventions. Another may just want to become absorbed in writing or in playing a musical instrument. This is very much an individual thing. Self-actualization is all about being fully who you are, and we are all different.

The achievement of this level of satisfaction depends both on the choices we make and on the vagaries of happenstance. We should be careful what directions to choose, such as whom to marry and which career to pursue. But it is not entirely up to us. Fate can take a hand in the form of ill health or injury, as well as unexpected boosts to our good fortune such as a financial windfall or being in the right place at the right time. Take Kate Middleton. When she enrolled at university it is possible that, like other young women, she dreamed of meeting a suitable man who would become her partner but she could not possibly have anticipated that it would be the future king.

It is important to recognize potential hazards as well as opportunities when they arise and to have enough self-knowledge to be able to recognise what would truly make us happy.

CHAPTER 9

Intrinsic Values

This is often referred to as the spiritual need, where the word 'spiritual' is used in its broadest sense covering all forms of motivation which transcend the individual's personal interests. Consequently it is also sometimes referred to by the alternative title 'Self-Transcendence'[1]. This emphasizes the contrast with all previous levels in the Hierarchy each of which involves some form of self-interest, but at this level of motivation one is inspired by ideals which lie beyond the boundaries of one's own personal needs and which are pursued altruistically.

Here are found aesthetics, compassion, ethical standards, a love of beauty and of nature. It also includes those drives which impel us to pursue causes like justice, the welfare of the poor, preservation of the environment, and social equality, as well as religious beliefs.

It may look as if intrinsic values are, by definition, always good and beneficial but this is not the case. Just like all the other levels this one has its downside too. Take honour. At first sight this seems fine and in many contexts so it is. But consider honour killings. We could also cite the Christian burning of witches, the Nazis' value of racial purity which led to the holocaust and other horrors, and the cruel ideologies of Al-Qaeda and Islamic State.

This brings us to motivation by religious faith. On the one hand these belief systems ostensibly encourage high moral standards including tolerance and the performance of charitable works. But on the other hand they can be used by the unscrupulous to persuade people to follow destructive paths such as religious wars, suppression of minorities, and terrorism. Double standards have been going on since historical records first appeared and show no sign of disappearing.

In fact values are personal even though they tend to arise from a culture which is shared. Two people do not have to uphold the same principles in spite of the tendency towards conformity within any given community. For example one may value the sanctity of life and condemn assisted suicide for the terminally ill while another values compassion and upholds mercy killing.

As far as we know this is the only motivational category which has no aspect at all that is shared with another species. Maslow believed this could be said of self-actualization[2], but recent research into the behaviour of primates suggests that he was mistaken in this belief. In my view if they are healthy, free and inhabiting an environment which adequately provides their needs, then they aspire to living life to the full according to their own kind and are therefore motivated to self-actualize.

Our pet dogs and cats, if well treated, healthy and loved, also live life to the full according to their own natures. For them also this is self-actualization. But they do not have a sense of values. A dog's loyalty to master or mistress is out of a sense of belonging and esteem for the 'pack leader' and not as an intrinsic value.

It is only the ability to be motivated by a sense of values which distinguishes us from the most advanced of other living creatures. That is why it is important to include this particular level in any theory of human motivation. Maslow's popularised earlier version of the Hierarchy of Needs stops at self-actualization, and in my view denies us our humanity.

As a result of the current spread of eastern meditation practices in the west, some transpersonalists maintain that the human race is in the process of evolving yet more levels to the hierarchy, namely those higher states of consciousness which meditation can produce.

I disagree. The seven levels of the Motivation Hierarchy are not states of consciousness but categories of motivating needs. They are as different as chalk and cheese so the addition of states of consciousness onto the top of the Hierarchy is a category error.

Meditation practice and the desire to attain an associated altered state of consciousness, are motivated by the aim to transcend the self. This is motivation by an intrinsic value. There is no need for any more levels to accommodate the aspiration to reach higher states of consciousness.

It is undoubtedy true that in the ages to come *homo sapiens* will evolve into *homo something else*, provided we do not destroy ourselves with atomic warfare and planetary pollution in the meantime. It may well be that this new species will have evolved another category of motivation beyond intrinsic values. But we, *homo sapiens*, cannot possibly envisage what that level will be any more than a chimpanzee can understand motivation by intrinsic values.

CHAPTER 11

Childhood

It is well known that the first few years of childhood are the most important in determining character and personality. What may not be so well known is how the development of a child's experience mirrors our species' evolutionary history as described in chapter 1.

The story starts in the womb. With the first cell division survival is established. The foetus's physiological needs are supplied by the placenta and the first onslaught on safety is normally the trauma of birth. A mother-child bond of belonging is established via touch and eye contact. When it comes to potty-training and learning to walk and talk, parental approval is an experience of esteem.

More lessons are learned when interacting with other infants. At school the sense of belonging and of esteem — or lack of these — are reinforced. Teachers and parents then encourage children to express their individuality and to develop skills including those at which they appear to excel (self-actualization). Finally society's moral values are inculcated, both by direct instruction and indirectly via example, making use of suitable stories such as those in which perseverance is rewarded and good triumphs over evil.

All of this happens in the first few years. The Jesuits are reputed to have claimed: 'Give us a child until seven years of age and it will be ours for life' — a shrewd observation.

The younger the child the more impressionable it is because the ability to assess critically what is happening to oneself is slow to develop. In the earliest years experiences go straight into the unconscious as if it were a sponge soaking them up, and the slightest upset in any one of these early developmental stages can have a lasting effect since the experience cannot yet be monitored by the faculty of reason. In this way programmes become installed in the unconscious and stay there, ready to be triggered at any time in the form of reactionary behaviour.

Take the toddler who stumbles into the wall and his parents laugh.

From the parents' point of view this is an amusing sight to watch and is soon forgotten. But for the child it is a blow both to his sense of belonging and to his need for parental approval (esteem). A few more experiences like this and he may grow up with a lack of self-confidence and a mistrust of authority figures, both of which will affect his ability to relate to others in an appropriate way.

Consider the child who proudly brings home from school an example of her work, perhaps a painting. Yes, it is a crude daub, but if it is criticised by Mum or Dad or by a beloved older sibling the blow to her self-esteem and to her willingness to put effort into achievement, can be crushing. Such experiences could have a lasting effect on her ability to sustain a career.

Whenever an infant experiences one of these mishaps, an immediate loving and reassuring hug by Mum or Dad is vital to alleviate the damaging effect. This way the child's unconscious memory will couple the hurt with that which makes it all better again and hopefully any lasting deleterious effect will have been averted. At the same time self-confidence has been encouraged in the belief that hurtful experiences can be dealt with.

The next hazardous environment is the school playground where sadly bullying has become endemic. This is one of the scourges of growing up in today's society and can seriously affect the victim's willingness to mix and bond (belonging) because it makes relationships of any kind seem dangerous. It destroys self-confidence (esteem).

What is the process by which these early experiences have such an impact on the formation of character and personality? The short answer is the power of association.

Before the onset of the ability to think logically and to reason a young child is programmed to learn by association. Babies' first movements are completely unco-ordinated, but then they learn to associate certain physical sensations with the ability to reach out towards objects. From among the sounds they can produce with their mouths they learn to associate the sound 'mama' with the person into whose face they gaze so often. There is also the matter of learning to stand upright and walk, which again are done at a purely instinctive level by trial and error, getting to associate certain sensations and movements with the desired result. What is learned is then retained in unconscious memory and, once learned, each skill becomes automatic.

This essential programme to learn by association has its downside as we can learn the wrong things. Take two-year-old Rose who was playing in the living-room with her toy farmyard animals. She slipped, banged her head against the wall and ended up lying on the carpet still clutching her toy cow. Mum, who was upstairs at the time, heard crying and came downstairs to pick Rose up and give her a hug. But the association between cow and being hurt and alone had already been established by the delay in mother's arrival, and so it remained as a programme. In later adult life she dislikes cows without having any idea as to why. It is useless telling her that cows are gentle creatures as that has no bearing whatsoever on the content of her unconscious memory.

Rex was six and had a brother Guy who was four. Guy could be annoying and Rex found he could deal with his sibling by hitting him. At an unconscious level Rex learned to associate hitting out with being annoyed and Guy learned to associate his own frustrations with domination by another. So Rex is now unconsciously programmed to lash out in order to get his own way, frequently getting into brawls, while Guy has grown into a rebellious teenager with a distaste for anyone exercising authority or wielding power.

Programmes are not just something that a few unfortunate people have. We all have them lurking in the dark depths of our memories, ready and waiting to erupt in reactionary behaviour whenever a trigger occurs.[1] Well might we say: 'I don't know what came over me'.

When once we reach that stage in childhood at which reason begins to operate, this automatic formation of programmes by association is not so powerful, but nevertheless it can still happen if the experience is strong enough. Some years ago when already in my sixties I tripped over onto the pavement and chipped my shoulder bone[2]. I lay there stupefied while passers-by stood over me. My father's advice came into my head: 'In an accident get the exact location of where it happened.' The fact that he had actually been referring to car accidents did not occur to me at that moment, so in a daze I asked for a detail to locate where I was. Somebody said: 'You are by a grating.' However at that precise moment it so happened that I was looking at a manhole cover in the pavement by my feet and an association was formed. Guess what? In the days after the accident I kept on calling manhole covers 'gratings' in spite of knowing they were not.

When we suffer a trauma there is a temporary regression to the helplessness and dependency of infancy together with the accompanying process of learning by association. We soon snap out of it, but in the meantime all sorts of associated links can be made and fed into the unconscious mind. Fortunately I was able to trace back this particular association to its origin and thereby release it. Otherwise I would probably still be calling manhole covers 'gratings' and either trying to conceal this mental quirk or endeavouring to laugh it off.

What has all this to tell us about becoming parents ourselves? As adults we can avail ourselves of advice, but this does not prevent us from being motivated to behave spontaneously when something buried in the unconscious is triggered.

Young Tom's father had a sense of humour and used to play practical jokes at his son's expense for his own amusement. He meant no harm but was unaware either of his own programme to be amused by another's discomfort or of his son's sense of humiliation and ridicule — a violation of Tom's need for esteem from his primary role model, his own father. Laughing *at* a child is quite different form laughing *with* a child.

Moreover Tom was learning by association how fathers behave. So now he has children of his own a programme to ridicule them keeps on being triggered. It is how we *perceive* a situation that gets implanted so that it can come to the surface later on, and this last example is of the 'taking it out on someone else' syndrome.

From time to time we come across people reacting inappropriately or out of proportion to the situation. In these circumstances it can usually be guaranteed that they are actually reacting, not to the current event but to something else, possibly a programme formed during childhood or a delayed reaction to something that occurred earlier that same day.

What I am trying to get across in this chapter is the vulnerability of children, especially the very young, when it comes to a violation of any one of their basic human needs. Parenting is an enormous responsibility and no-one can get it absolutely right. We just have to do our best. Hopefully some knowledge of the Hierarchy will help parents to understand where their children are coming from, while at the same time maintaining their own authority as their children's main role models and objects of esteem. Psychologists refer to 'good-enough parenting' and realistically that is the best we can hope to achieve.

CHAPTER 12

Deficiency

The word 'need' implies that consequences may follow if there is serious under-fulfilment. When teenagers turn to violence or drugs questions are asked as to what went wrong, the assumption being that somehow they must have missed out on some essential influence in their earlier years — and indeed this is sometimes the case.

One possible consequence of a serious deficiency is to get one's motivation stuck in that particular overwhelming drive as if it can never be satisfied. So those who suffered a period of starvation some time in the past might subsequently be unable to curb their appetites. A child who was not loved might become an adult who craves friendship in a demanding and possessive way but never feels content. The child who was forever being criticised might grow into an adult who strives excessively in competition with others to gain recognition and yet never feels confident. The hallmark of a deficiency need is that a person becomes stuck in a groove, forever seeking satisfaction of a particular need despite many instances of its fulfilment.

People affected in this way are vulnerable and open to manipulation by those who are unscrupulous. An example of this can be seen in the current problem of radicalisation of men within our prisons, the recruitment of inmates to join groups that support terrorism. As soon as their term of imprisonment comes to an end and they are released they immediately become a danger to the rest of society.

How can this radicalization be so easily achieved? First of all a prison population is going to include a large number of men who have missed out on the need to *belong*. The mere fact of their being inside demonstrates to them that they are rejected by society and they have responded by distancing themselves in turn. In fact they may revel in the reputation of being hard. So along comes a group of equally hard individuals, welcoming them and addressing them as 'brother'. This approach is irresistible as it taps straight into their deficiency in the need to belong without violating their own self-image of being tough.

The next step is to treat them as valuable members of the group who can achieve great things when once freed from prison. This feeds their need for *esteem*. What are those great things? Criminal acts of violence, in other words what they are already used to doing but now for a purpose and with approval. The fact that they are capable of acts of violence confirms the possibility of achievement, self-fulfilment, *self-actualization* — and all that simply with the skills and life-style they have already embraced. Finally this can all be perpetrated in the name of a cause which becomes their over-riding *intrinsic value*.

This whole radicalization process has simply followed a steady climb up the Motivation Hierarchy, starting at the level of their deficiency need.

Determining what can be done to prevent this pattern of grooming is not easy. There have been instances in which a prison padre has approached an inmate with a brotherly approach and succeeded in converting him to follow the intrinsic value of Christian love. But such instances are not common, and in any case are unlikely to work with someone whose background is in a different culture.

The cure has to be something that feeds the need for brotherhood while at the same time utilizing their macho image. This has sometimes worked with young offenders who have been encouraged to join together to play football or enrol in a boxing club, giving them a means of occupying their time, a channel for their hormones, and goals to achieve which are compatible with a macho self-image. An essential ingredient in this approach is the presence of a suitable role model the youngsters can respect.

Another example of exploitation is a scandal recently revealed in some of our cities, namely the widespread sexual abuse of vulnerable young girls who are also short on the satisfaction of their need for love and to belong. So they are approached by men who offer gifts and affection to which they are easy prey. Once hooked the girls are then abused.

In both of these situations, namely grooming for radicalization and for sexual exploitation, the only solution is to give those who are at risk a sense of belonging to, and pride in, the wider community whatever their ethnic or religious background. In other words the negativity of their experience at the level of belonging must be counteracted by something positive. Of course this is easier said than done.

The necessary remedial input needs to be accomplished before they actually get into trouble, and possibly at school. Also young people need to be educated in the techniques of grooming so that they are forewarned and can recognise when they are being targeted.

It remains to be seen whether today's tendency to communicate via an electronic tablet instead of face to face, will create another kind of belonging deficiency. Maybe the need will be satisfied by being a member of an internet social group, but to me this feels unreal as well as unsafe. This is communication with a representation of a person, not an actual person. Let us hope that my fears are unfounded and that 'good-enough parenting' will have a stronger lasting influence than these artificial technological contacts.

One cannot leave the topic of deficiency without mentioning sublimation. This can occur when a deficiency cannot be rectified and instead the sufferer puts all of his or her energies into the pursuit of another drive at a higher level. It is a deliberate reversal of natural pre-potency[1]. When someone is killed in a road accident or dies at a young age from an incurable disease, family members may deal with their loss and grief by campaigning for safer road conditions or by setting up a charitable fund for medical research into a cure. Their belonging need is sublimated by conversion into the pursuit of an intrinsic value relevant to their loss.

Another example is those who, despite having lost limbs, pursue self-fulfilment and success in paralympic sports. Clearly these deliberate reversals of needs pre-potency take considerable courage and determination.

Sometimes the deficiency experience can be so devastating that it over-rides the pre-potency of lower levels on the hierarchy, resulting in self-harm and suicide. The motive to survive is no longer predominant.

The wish to die is also passionately expressed by those who suffer physically and mentally, either from a terminal illness or from a crippling disability. Either their incapacity makes them unable to fulfil this wish for themselves, or the law means that they feel unable to ask someone else to do it for them.

In my opinion it reveals a misunderstanding of human nature and of logic to argue that because there are cases of sublimation therefore the law should continue to condemn assisted suicide for the relief of suffering. But that is an opinion not shared by those whose values are different from my own and who seemingly rate the sanctity of human life above compassion for those who suffer. This compassion is shown to our animals but is considered to be a dangerous solution when offered to fellow humans.

CHAPTER 13

Multiple Motives

On asking the question: 'Why did I do that?' the obvious answer may not be the correct one. Have we chosen from the head or the heart? Has there been an influence of which we are unaware?

We pride ourselves on being rational, but consider the number of assault cases that come before the courts in which the perpetrator has just suddenly lashed out, or those choices of marriage partner which end in divorce because some characteristic of the other person was not taken into account when in love. And then there are the compulsive gamblers who are convinced that the odds are bound to turn in their favour sooner rather than later.

The choice between competing needs of equal strength can be tricky. Take an army sergeant major. His job is to mould his soldiers into an effective working and fighting team. He has to encourage bonding while maintaining his own authority in order to satisfy his superiors. Parents also experience a similar dilemma in trying to get the balance right between love (*belonging*) and authority (*esteem*).

Surely we must all have experienced occasions when competing motives have battled inside us producing inaction like an internal traffic jam. Shakespeare's Hamlet was torn between the desire to avenge his father's murder and his need to verify the authenticity of the accusation with the result that he missed a number of opportunities to act. Do we tell a frail old lady who is dying that her son has just suffered a serious road accident? Truth v compassion, both are intrinsic values. Does a woman leave her cruel husband and take their children with her to an uncertain future? Which is the greater risk to their safety and security?

Sometimes we think we have chosen a course of action for reason A when in fact a stronger motivation B lurked unawares at the back of our minds. Recently Jane bought some fabric she liked in order to make a tunic. But something kept nagging her. The material was nothing special so why did she like it? Weeks later the answer hit home. The pattern and colour closely resembled that of a tunic she had worn some years earlier for a demonstration of jive which elicited enthusiastic applause at an event run by the local dancing school. In other words the fabric had triggered a memory of success, a motivation to buy which took precedence over its moderate aesthetic appeal. In this instance the unconscious drive was benign but her choice could hardly be described as 'informed'.

On the plus side there are those so-called 'lucky' moments when we choose on a hunch and it turns out to have been the best choice we could have made. I suspect this is the basis on which most women would choose the home in which they wish to live, whether it has the right feel and atmosphere, while the man would consider whether it is convenient and at the right price.

In fact this is not a bad basis on which to choose between alternatives. First consult the heart and intuition by imagining each possible outcome in turn. This brings likes and dislikes to the surface and reveals preferences. The next step is to consult the head by considering whether the preferred option raises any negative issues. This is like creating a short list and then narrowing it down to one, and provides a

good chance that the final decision will turn out to have been the right one because both head and heart have contributed.

By contrast consider the unfortunate marriage of Prince Charles to Diana Spencer. With hindsight it is clear that he had been persuaded by head arguments to conform to the royal tradition of marrying a suitable virgin who could provide an indisputable heir to the throne. His heart was over-ridden in favour of his duty (*intrinsic value*) and also possibly because of pressure from family elders (*esteem*). Diana on the other hand clearly had a romantic vision of marrying her prince and looked forward to living happily ever after (*belonging* and *self-actualization*). Presumably she was unaware that this was a fairy-tale vision and as a result it ruled her head. She seems to have taken no thought concerning the real-life traditions of royalty and whether they would suit her.

Choosing a career is another important decision which can be affected by different urges. On the head level: What are my particular talents and skills? Can I afford the requisite training? Will the income provide a satisfactory livelihood? On the heart level: What do I really enjoy doing? Am I being influenced by friends' choices or by family preferences? Is my temperament suited to a particular choice? Is the thought of the length of training putting me off? Many a person has chosen the easy or the obvious option only to regret it later.

Do we really understand why we choose the people to whom to give our votes during an election? Have we really considered all the options presented by the various candidates and political parties, or do we just vote for a particular party out of habit or family tradition regardless of the candidate's own personal record? Do we confuse national and local issues when electing our local councillors?

CHAPTER 14

Curiosity

The young of all mammalian species have a lot to learn before they mature, and their willingness to do so is fuelled by curiosity without which their mothers' lessons might go unheeded. Even as adults many species continue to display inquisitiveness. Meerkats whose lives have been portrayed in detail on our TV screens, will investigate anything new to find out if it is a threat or is edible, and the Rock of Gibraltar's apes are an absolute nuisance to tourists with their insatiable and intrusive attentions.

Human infants are no different. Toddlers get everywhere. They will explore the contents of a cupboard, drawer, handbag with all the enthusiasm of someone who has discovered a priceless treasure. Then comes the stage of asking endless questions: 'Where do babies come from?', 'Why do men grow hair on their chins?', 'Why does the moon not fall out of the sky?', 'How do birds fly?', and so it goes on.

In my childhood a grandmother clock[1] hung above the fireplace in the living room. I wanted to know how to tell the time, so my father sat me on his knee and explained: 'Do you see two hands, one longer than the other, and twelve numbers around the edge of the dial? Well,………….. '. I remember that occasion clearly as it resulted in an intense sense of accomplishment as the new knowledge was absorbed and later applied.

Human progress has been fuelled by our sense of curiosity, the urge to explore and discover new lands, to find out more about the world in which we live, the stars and the cosmos, as well as what goes on in that world inside our minds.

The grand scheme of things is not the only target of our curiosity. We try to figure out how some artefact works in order to be able to make use of it. This may entail studying a book of instructions for the control panel of a new central heating system, or poring over a diagram before trying to assemble a chair that has arrived in a flat-pack. Curiosity is also responsible for gossip with the person next door as we seek to find out what we can about the neighbours.

During my childhood most people took their holidays in this country at the seaside with the intention of enjoying a relaxed break from routine, but now the fashion is to go abroad, see new places, try foreign foods, come into contact with new customs and observe un-familiar wildlife in its natural surroundings.

The producers of TV programmes give us ongoing sitcoms because they know that, if hooked by one episode, our curiosity to find out what happens next will turn the series into compulsive viewing.

All branches of experimental science depend upon a desire to know what happens if we apply a certain force, mix two chemicals, or intro-duce an electric current. We send probes into the depths of the ocean and we explore the micro-world of an atom and the macro-world of space. We thirst for knowledge about the past, the history of the plan-et with its shifting continents, and civilizations that once existed but whose memory is now contained in ruins, bones and broken pottery.

It seems that curiosity is a major motivator, so where does it fit into the Hierarchy? Well, sometimes it doesn't as it may simply be a means to an end rather than an end in itself. In some of the examples quoted above, curiosity is not the need but is an activity motivated by a particular need, whether that be safety (is this food tasty and fit to eat?), belonging (is this person one with whom I can have a relationship?), self-esteem (can I learn this new skill?), self-actualization (what would this new direction offer to my career?).

It seems to me that it is only when curiosity is the pursuit of know-ledge and understanding for its own sake and not for any self-interested purpose that it can be said to be a motivation in its own right, where-upon it can be classified as an intrinsic value. This is what drives those scientists, archaeologists, naturalists, explorers, who are totally devoted to their work with the sole aim of discovering some fresh fact, some new explanation. This may also be what drives one to read to the end of a detective novel to find out who did it, or to experience a different culture by visiting a new holiday destination abroad.

In his original paper[2] of 1943 Maslow acknowledged that the pur-suit of knowledge for its own sake was missing from the Hierarchy as he had conceived it to be at that time. It was only by the later addition of intrinsic values that his work on motivation theory was completed.

CHAPTER 15

The Urge To Fit In

We all need family and friends and want a congenial atmosphere at work, and in order to achieve satisfactory relationships we have to learn how to fit in. The learning process usually starts with accepting the authority of parents and teachers. Without this basic grounding when young a person will probably never be able fully to integrate into society which inevitably has to be organized with leaders, bosses, police, law courts and accepted rules of behaviour to avoid anarchy.

Teenage rebelliousness is a natural stage in the transition from childhood to becoming an adult. One is shaking off parental authority but not yet acclimatized to adult responsibilities. However the earlier example of parents as role models kicks in as we mature.

What one was taught to accept as a matter of course when young, has a tendency to remain so. When I was quite small my mother encouraged me to clean and tidy my own bedroom, but would not let me cook during wartime in order to avoid wastage of meagre rations. Consequently I grew up naturally tidy but cooking always feels like a burdensome chore. The point is that such practices have to be encouraged when the child is still young enough to be uncritical and desirous of being trusted with a grown-up task. If parents wait until later before introducing chores and other desirable activities then these will come across as an imposition.

My mother was born just before the nineteenth century gave way to the twentieth. During her lifetime it became socially acceptable for women to go out to work — but only until they got married when they were expected to take upon themselves the roles of looking after the home and raising children. In fact when I was at school women teachers were still obliged to resign their jobs if they married.

My mother was brainy but intellectually starved for several years, having to spend her days engaged in small talk with no-one for company most of the time apart from her children. In spite of this she made a good job of it. One had to fit in with society's norms, and indeed children benefited from the undivided attention of their mothers.

Today the situation has changed, partly due to the fact that material standards of expectation have increased. The advertising industry ensures that children feel left out unless they have the latest toys, and teenagers must have the latest music, mobile phones and electronic gadgets, all of which cost money. In many homes it is the youngsters who call the shots.

In order to be able to afford the life-style that advertisers persuade us is the norm, many families find that both parents have to go out to work while leaving the older children unsupervised and the young at a nursery. This makes families in which the mother stays at home to care for the young, feel poor by comparison because they cannot provide the luxuries that others regard as normal. Yet the irony is that they may still be enjoying a standard of living better than that of their grandparents.

Peer pressure has replaced 'What will the neighbours think?' and 'Keeping up with the Joneses' has acquired new strengths. The needs for belonging and esteem now focus upon possessions whereas formerly the emphasis was on acceptable behaviour. Family life appears to have become commercialized.

Then there is 'getting in with the wrong crowd'. Teenagers are at the stage of exploring the adult world of independence without any previous experience of its pitfalls, while parental advice may evoke resentment. This leaves them wide open to influences from others whom they trust. As a result many youngsters have found themselves on the wrong side of the law after falling in with a new set of friends.

This predilection to fit in, to belong, can usurp levels higher up the Hierarchy by its pre-potency[1]. Take religious faith, an aspect of intrinsic values. Most of us derive our fundamental beliefs in childhood from parents, teachers and the wider culture in which we were raised. We accept without question what is taught by those in authority and who are respected, so that attitudes and beliefs become ingrained.

Yes, there are those who question their faith when they have acquired sufficient reasoning capacity and knowledge of the world, and there are those who feel guilty for daring to question what their culture regards as *a priori* truth. But the vast majority keep what was absorbed in childhood, especially whatever became firmly embedded at an age before reason kicked in and is then reinforced in adulthood by their community and culture.

In this way beliefs are handed down from generation to generation, to survive long after the circumstances which gave rise to them have been forgotten. Take the religious ban against eating pork. To the ancients in the Middle East this was a very sensible prohibition because pork goes off quickly in a hot climate. But now that their descendants are spread across the globe and have access to modern refrigerators, one wonders why pork should still be considered unclean.

This handing down of beliefs and attitudes is also true for political affiliations. We tend to find families and indeed neighbourhoods in which most people support one particular party and going against the grain is perceived as disloyal.

Of course peer pressure can be beneficial. A shy girl can be persuaded by her friends to come out of her shell by plucking up courage to accompany them to a party or disco. A young man who was bottom of the class at school might be encouraged to join his local football team or gymnasium. Many of us would never have embarked upon a path which turned out successful had not someone strongly urged that we give it a try and join in.

Being able to fit in is important for a satisfactory social life, as those who stand out by being different will know to their cost. Prejudice can be very unpleasant to bear and is an expression of the downside of the motivation to belong. The very concept of belonging creates a boundary between those who do and those who do not, whether the difference be racial, social, religious or whatever. It all comes down to identity.

In summary, fitting in is basically motivated by the need to belong. However there can also be an element of fear concerning possible adverse repercussions resulting from nonconformity (safety need), or the desire to be liked and respected (esteem).

CHAPTER 16

Guilt and Shame

Guilt is when we feel bad about having violated our own values and shame is when we have violated the values of our community. The opposite of guilt is innocence and the opposite of shame is honour. Confession usually helps alleviate the feeling of guilt but only makes shame worse. So, for example, a woman who has been raped may keep the fact to herself out of a sense of shame while fully aware that she has done no wrong.

In a multicultural society a clash of values is inevitable, especially for the children of immigrant parents. They meet with two different sets of values at home and at school, sometimes with tragic consequences. The young Asian girl who falls in love and refuses to marry the man chosen by her parents, violates their honour and causes them shame. She may face the danger of becoming a victim of honour killing in spite of the fact that our laws and customs are on her side.

On the other hand consider the husband who has an affair with another woman and feels guilty about deceiving his wife. Our society tends to regard such marital transgressions as unfortunate but not unlawful. Unless he is a member of a strict religious congregation he is unlikely to experience public shame should the facts become known.

Homosexuality is no longer illegal in the UK but many gay men still find it difficult to come out because of the anticipated shame within their families and communities. Past attitudes have not entirely gone away in spite of the fact that this no longer carries a guilty verdict in the courts. Alan Turing's conviction, treatment and subsequent suicide, followed by the more recent revelation of his invaluable contribution to this country during the war by breaking the Enigma code, seem to have produced a sense of communal guilt. The reason it took more than half a century for his code-breaking work at Bletchley Park to be revealed was the oath of secrecy taken by all who worked there[1], assiduously observed for several decades after the war came to an end.

An attempt to inflict shame can be used as a punishment for guilt. I can remember when school-children who misbehaved were punished by having to stand in a corner in front of the rest of the class. In the more distant past every village had its stocks, and miscreants could spend a day fastened into one of those contraptions while neighbours pelted them with rotten vegetables.

For children feelings of guilt and shame can be particularly acute. What is often not appreciated by parents and teachers is that there is a world of difference to a child between being told: 'That was naughty' and 'You are naughty'. The former refers to a particular guilty act in the recent past for which one can say 'sorry' and be forgiven. A lesson has been learned. However the latter is a shaming statement about one's very identity, one's soul. One is labelled 'naughty' as if a tag has been hung around one's neck and which will stay there forever. Worse still, perhaps, is to be told 'You are bad'. Messages like this can become embedded in the child's psyche and accepted as a self-description, causing all sorts of problems in adulthood from wimpishness to criminality. After all, if one is bad then one might as well behave badly.

What have these feelings to do with the Hierarchy? A guilty feeling is primarily a loss of self-esteem because one has let oneself down in terms of one's own values. A burglar is guilty in the eyes of the law but it is unlikely he feels guilty because respect for the property of others clearly is not one of his values.

It is said that confession is good for the soul, and indeed getting it off one's chest frequently produces a sense of release from guilt even if there is punishment to follow. A burden shared is a burden halved.

Shame is more deep-rooted. It entails the feeling of being cut off, not just from certain other people who are expected to disapprove for a while until one is forgiven or the incident forgotten, but condemned by everyone in one's own community and forever. One is an outcast. One no longer belongs because shared intrinsic values have been violated. These values have been passed on from generation to generation and have become entrenched with assumed inviolable authority and therefore not to be questioned. The offender has been placed outside the boundaries of his or her own culture and society and is likely to remain there. Forgiveness is not an option. One no longer belongs.

CHAPTER 17

Sex

Every adult will recognize the power of the sexual drive. It is an instinct as old as the hills and without it no animal species, including humans, would survive. It has come to us through the processes of evolution and is embedded in our genes.

Since the urge results from stimulation of hormones it is firmly rooted at the physiological level of motivation, regardless of whatever else it was that promoted the hormonal rush in any specific instance.

It is so strong and so universal that Sigmund Freud gave sex prime importance in his psychoanalytic theories. Modern psychology now disputes some of his conclusions but nevertheless its power to motivate is undeniable. Because it manifests at the physiological level, in terms of pre-potency it is preceded only by the will to survive.

Sex tends to get confused with love because ideally it takes place within a loving relationship, but the two are not the same. This is made clear by acts of rape, prostitution, and one-night stands, all of which stem from the sexual urge and have nothing to do with love. The phrase 'to make love' can mislead.

Confusion is also compounded by the romantic concept of love at first sight which is fed to young girls in stories like Sleeping Beauty and Cinderella. This kind of initial experience of attraction cannot be anything but hormonal since the two parties are completely ignorant of each others' characters and mutual love has not yet had a chance to blossom.

There is, of course, erotic love which combines sex with relationship and this will be included in the next chapter. Here we are concerned with the sex drive which is purely physiological and is shared with other mammals.

Throughout mammalian species it appears to be strongest in the male since it is he who has to take the active role. It is he who has to have an erection and inject sperm. All the female needs to do is passively accept provided she is in season. Consequently males court the females and compete with each other for the privilege.

All this have humans inherited from our evolutionary ancestors — except for the bit about being 'in season'. Traditionally it has been commonly recognized as fitting for a man to take the initiative by seeking out the woman of his choice and then for her to say yea or nay rather than the other way around. If he had a rival they might well have come to blows or even fought a duel.

she is mine!

However in the industrial world society's attitudes and customs are changing. Men and women are taking on each others' traditional roles with women going out to work and men being urged to develop their feminine sides, not only by sharing in the tasks of child-rearing but also by revealing their softer emotions. Women are becoming more proactive sexually with men facing what feels like an assault upon their dominant macho self-image. These changes are driven mostly by the collective motivation amongst women to realise their needs for esteem and self-actualization.

In all of this what seem to be in danger of being overlooked are the needs of the children who are produced by the sexual act. We must ensure that promotion of equality does not end up depriving infants of much-needed maternal care and love, even if this has to be provided by someone other than the mother.

Centuries ago societies observed that the sexual drive had its problems and countered this by laying down rules governing the sexual act, such as a ban on incest. An exception was the Egyptian pharaohs who tended to marry a sister in order to maintain the dynastic line. However they paid the inevitable price, suffering inherited physical and medical problems.

In the days when the world was sparsely populated people were encouraged to 'go forth and multiply'. This edict was attributed to God rather than to an enlightened leader and so it became a religious imperative. Religions tend to ignore the passage of time and changing circumstances and the fact that what was desirable in one age may become disastrous in another. Today this ancient value has become set in stone. It is upheld in certain faiths by a ban on the use of contraceptives and the failure to promote smaller families, thereby displaying a total disregard for changing circumstances and the fact that earth's resources can no longer cope in the face of ever increasing over-population.

If the human race continues to expand this will soon lead to devastating consequences in terms of overcrowding and wars over dwindling resources, mainly water, food and power. The lower needs will perforce exert their pre-potency. Every society needs to review its cultural and religious values concerning sex and reproduction right now if the human species and the planet on which we live are to survive into the future.

CHAPTER 18

Power and Love

Archetypes

Examination of the mythology, legends and folk tales of various cultures, both past and present, reveals certain themes which are common to all and keep on recurring[1]. These include the hero's journey, hidden treasure, rags to riches, a wise person, the underworld, and the triumph of good over evil. But the most common themes of all are power and love.

Such stories endure, for they not only serve to prepare the young for adult life by inculcating the mores of their culture but also reinforce the culture's mores for the adults.

The hero's journey encourages us to strive in life to reach fulfilment (*self-actualization*). A treasure might represent either the rewards of success (*esteem* and *self-actualization*) or the attainment of perfection within one's soul (*intrinsic values*). A wise person can suggest to the young that they should respect their elders (*esteem*) or it can be symbolic of one's own intuitive inner wisdom to which one should give heed for guidance (*intrinsic values*). The underworld is a warning about programmes that can well up from the depths of the unconscious in response to a hidden version of any one of the motivating drives.[2]

The two themes which occur most frequently, namely power and love, are the most complex. Every religion and mythology I can think of has some representation of these two archetypal forces[3], from Mars and Venus, Ra and Hathor, to Jehovah and the Virgin Mary. In folk tales power can be represented by a beneficent ruler or a tyrant as well as by animals with strength such as lions and buffalo, and love is represented in all its forms from maternal love and friendship to unrequited love and betrayal.

Even in the most primitive of cultures we find beliefs and legends about Father Sky and Mother Earth. The Sky was powerful. It could pour down floods and create havoc with storms and lightning as well as causing droughts by withholding life-giving rain. The Earth nurtured and grew plants for food after being fertilized by water from the Sky, but it could also be wrathful, unleashing earthquakes and volcanoes.

These two important archetypal forces have a biological basis and are present in the psyche of every human being. They are the product of evolution and indeed it is not difficult to trace their emergence up the evolutionary tree. Amongst mammals the two most important social drives are the struggle for dominance and care of the young.

Clearly power and love motivate our thoughts, decisions and actions, so if the Motivation Hierarchy is complete as claimed, then they must appear somewhere in its structure. Well, yes they do, but both have so many different forms of expression that they can appear at almost any of the different levels.

Power

In its basic form power is simply the exercise of physical strength, whether to impress or to overcome another. The former is an expression of the need for esteem. The latter, however, could be more complicated. Why would anyone wish to defeat another in a show of strength?

A sudden spontaneous bout of fisticuffs is the result of some need having been violated. It might be that the other man has pulled out a knife and threatens one's life (*survival* and *safety*), has designs on one's wife (*belonging*), has used insulting language (*esteem*), cheated at a card game (*self-actualization* and *intrinsic value*), or has heaped scorn upon one's most cherished belief (*intrinsic value* and *esteem*).

Sexual abuse and rape are recognised to be manifestations of a desire to exercise power over another. Domestic violence can be occasioned by a variety of similar motivations, but often these also entail a deficiency need[4] in the psychological make-up of the perpetrator, or something in his or her past which has left its mark in the form of a programme.

A preplanned show of physical strength such as in a boxing match or a strong-man competition, is for the kudos of winning (*esteem* and *self-actualization*). In this category we can also include power one stage removed, as in car racing in which it is not one's own physical power which is on display but that of the machine which the driver controls and with which he identifies.

Power can be social rather than physical, as in a ruler, leader, employer, or role model, and it is in this category that women can hold their own. Rulers command armies and police forces to maintain their positions, so physical force is present but at arm's length from the person at the top. The motivation for holding onto and exercising this kind of power may be a sense of duty and tradition (*intrinsic value*) or personal gratification (*self-actualization*) or the satisfaction of being held in high regard (*esteem*).

We are familiar with the lure of power, whether it be as president of a country, boss of a business, army general, member of parliament, terrorist, leader of a street gang, or simply the chairman of a local committee, and unless wisely-handled power can corrupt. 'Power tends to corrupt and absolute power corrupts absolutely',[5] a tendency portrayed accurately in George Orwell's allegory 'Animal Farm'.

Would-be revolutionaries beware! By deposing the old order you create a power vacuum which unanticipated power-seekers will endeavour to fill. Al-Qaeda usurped the revolution in Syria. Islamic State seeks to take over Iraq following the overthrow of Saddam Hussein and now Syria as well. During the twentieth century several African countries found themselves in the hands of ruthless dictators after gaining freedom from their European rulers. Following the first World War the Communist revolution in Russia was meant to free the proletariat from oppression and poverty but instead resulted in countless deaths and imprisonments under a dictatorship which lasted for decades.

Power comes in many contexts. Our susceptibility to manipulation by someone in authority was demonstrated scientifically in the 1960's. In a famous experiment Stanley Milgram managed to persuade volunteers to inflict upon a group of actors what were purported to be ever-increasing electric shocks[6]. For many their respect for the experimenter's authority took precedence over any compassion for their supposed victims. That should have been expected because esteem is prepotent over intrinsic values.[7]

Let us not forget the psychological and emotional power exercised over others by accomplished manipulators and confidence tricksters, whose motivation could be wealth in order to live in style (*self-actualization*), or the satisfaction of having another person under one's thumb (*self-esteem*) examples of which include internet hackers and school bullies.

When a child, Harold's father controlled him with the threat of the cane — this was before it became illegal in the UK. On growing up

Harold now gets his own back on society, having discovered he can ma-nipulate others by winding them up. He finds out what the other person values and then talks scornfully about it until that person loses control and, as a result, self-respect. Harold has discovered his own power.

This same technique is also used by some television reporters who pester their subjects with provocative questions, presumably in the hope that they will lose their cool and provide the television team with an explosive story.

Love

In the English language this one word 'love' is used to cover a number of different meanings ranging from a mere liking as in 'I love strawberries and cream' to deepest commitment as in 'Greater love hath no man than this, that a man lay down his life for his friends.'[8] The first of these two meanings is trivial and will be ignored, concentrating instead on maternal love, filial love, bonding, affection, friendship, erotic love and compassion.

Every one of these involves the concept of *belonging*. In addition maternal and erotic loves both involve a *physiological* element associ-ated with hormonal activity, maternal and filial loves have a hint of duty (*intrinsic value*) sanctioned by one's culture (*esteem*). The establish-ment of a filial bond involves a sense of *safety* within the family, and compassion is clearly an *intrinsic value*.

Arguably the strongest and most enduring love is that of a mother for her child. This is hardly surprising since she nurtured the child for nine months inside her own body. What closer form of belonging can there be?

Just as power has its negative manifestations so too does love. Unrequited passion is a painful experience which is all too common. Other negatives which arise from the need to belong are feelings of rejection, abandonment and alienation, as well as jealousy, favour-itism and possessiveness. This last is characterised by a total focus on 'I want' and an absence of the concepts of giving and sharing. In other words it is a negative aspect of *self-actualization* taking over from *belonging*.

A frequently used strategy for coping with a sense of being un-loved, is comfort eating. Unconsciously a person reverts to childhood experience by identifying with two separate roles simultaneously, one of which is the needy child while the other is that of mother who demonstrates love by feeding the child. It is not surprising that more women than men resort to this dual-role solution.

Changing Roles

Nature has made men taller and stronger than women and filled them with testosterone, giving them a concept of power as part of their self-image. On the whole they like to drive fast cars, indulge in extreme sports, fire guns, and assume that their macho image is attractive to women. Or at least that is how masculinity is portrayed.

In the past men could exert their authority as heads of households making use of their superior strength and with the support of society's mores and rules of conduct. Domestic violence existed and was ignored because the man was given the legal right to rule. With today's changing attitudes felt, unconsciously perhaps, as a threat to their macho self-image, domestic violence by men against women is still all too common. We are also seeing the rise of violence by some masculinized women against their weaker men. Either way the need for self-esteem within a domestic situation is still being played out physically in terms of power.

Religion has been another factor supporting male dominance. Belief systems inculcate communal values, so here we have yet another motivational level (*values*) being used to support what is in fact hormonal and *physiological*. Outside the industrialized nations this is still very much the case with women held in a subject and inferior role. But even within the industrialized nations the hold of religion over gender issues has not gone away albeit slowly being undermined. Opposition to women priests is a case in point.

In the modern world women claim equal rights with men, but this is proving an uphill struggle because it is impossible to legislate against testosterone and superior physical strength. On the other hand men will need to find another way of boosting their self-esteem as their culturally supported macho image is gradually eroded.

The feminist movement has kept up a steady onslaught on male strongholds resulting in the growth of men's counselling groups and bonding exercises to counter the perceived loss of masculinity. Businesses provide paint-balling weekends, though their purpose to stimulate a sense of male identity and bonding may be undermined by the occasional woman employee opting to participate.

The campaign to achieve equality under the law and equality of opportunity in education and employment, are laudable aims and should not be confused with an attempt to feminize men and masculinize women. Yes, it is desirable for men to stop concealing their softer emotions and for women to become bolder and more proactive, but let us not take this to the extreme of a defiance of nature which can only lead to psychological suppression and ultimately to social disaster.

One way of restoring a male's self-image and therefore his self-esteem, is through the social and political power which comes with leadership and authority. Such roles are not confined to the realms of politics and industry for myriads of opportunities present themselves to ordinary people, whether it be by gaining promotion at work to a position of responsibility, captaining a sports club, organizing local events, or simply being the life and soul of the party. This is one more reason why women get squeezed out of these roles.

Why is it that most men would prefer to own a dog rather than a cat? A dog is a pack animal and, if suitably trained, will recognise its owner as pack leader. On the other hand cats base their activities on territory, not relationships. If a neighbour offers better food and comfort then off they go. Could it be that the apparent recent rise in the ownership of dangerous dogs reflects an attempt to boost the macho image?

Concluding Remarks

Within a family the two persons having most influence on the formation of an infant's psyche are its parents. So if they have been exercising their traditional roles the children will grow up with these two archetypes well embedded in unconsciousness, namely the power of authority associated mainly with father and nurturing love with mother.

Power and love are so important that if there is a serious deficiency need in either of them it can manifest in any one of a number of psychological conditions such as insatiable lust, sadism, and the desire to torture, as well as extreme possessiveness, the conviction of being unlovable, and hatred of society. A psychiatrist presented with such a case would investigate whether the patient's past included abuse or profound powerlessness at a physical or emotional level, an experience of perceived abandonment or alienation, or a denial of essential love and nurturing over a crucial period of development.

These two archetypal energies have enormous influence in all our lives, from programmes of automatic reaction that have become implanted into our own unconscious memories, to the actions and behaviour patterns that we encounter and have to deal with in others.

Foremost in these influences are our parents and how they carried out their roles. In the industrialized world these roles are changing. Women go out to work and many men share in the nurturing role of bringing up their children, and this must have its effect on the psyches of the next and future generations. It remains to be seen what impact this will have upon the collective psyche, and how the archetypal energies of power and love will manifest within individuals and society in the future.

CHAPTER 19

The Profit Motive

We live in a capitalist society. The basic idea is that an individual's work is rewarded with the means to purchase goods and services, the reward being commensurate with the nature of the work and the effort which was put into it. This fact of itself is neither good nor bad, but what makes it so is how it operates and is regulated in practice. In other words, the human factor.

Many businesses are run honestly and ethically. For example a small high street shop sells goods all of which have a recommended retail price. This means that there is a direct correlation between how much is sold and the profit therefrom. But not all small businesses operate in this way. Take the antique dealer. If he comes across a valuable item being sold cheaply by someone who does not appreciate its worth, he snaps it up and sells it on, making a profit.

Big businesses work quite differently. Their *raison d'etre* is to make as much money as possible for their shareholders. So it is not surprising that there is public resistance to state-owned enterprises like the National Health Service or the prison system employing private companies. The only way to ensure that profit does not become more important than the quality of service provided, is to have frequent inspections carried out by an independent body. Unfortunately the inspectors, too, are human and may fail to spot problems until they become blatantly obvious.

One way of maximising profits is to employ workers on a zero hours contract. This gives all the advantages to the employer since the employee is engaged only when there is work to be done. The unfortunate employee is not even satisfied at the level of safety since there is no security of employment from day to day.

Making a profit is all about furthering one's own career and being able to provide the best possible life-style for oneself and one's family. At the lower income levels the motivation is somewhere in the range safety, belonging, esteem. However for those fortunate people whose income adequately provides at the lower levels, the profit motive is about self-actualization, being able to fulfil ambitions, indulge in pleasurable activities, purchase beautiful and expensive objects, and this is where greed can take over if there is no strong counter-influence from the level of intrinsic values.

This is precisely what happened to cause scandals in the banking world at the beginning of the twenty-first century, resulting in a financial crisis of international proportions. In some cases it was an individual employee of a finance company who speculated unwisely hoping for a fat reward but ended up causing his firm to suffer huge losses. In other cases it was the entire company which engaged in unethical practices in order to boost profits.

A large proportion of crime is motivated by the desire to make money quickly and with little effort although with some risk. During the Easter bank holiday long weekend in April 2015 a gang carried out the most daring and lucrative bank heist of all time when they broke into the safety deposit vault used by local jewellery merchants in

London's Hatton Garden district. They abseiled down the lift shaft to gain access and made off with jewellery worth mouth-watering millions of pounds.

Then there are the scammers who telephone unsuspecting victims out of the blue to announce that they have inherited a large legacy provided they send a certain sum of money to secure it, and the dodgy builders who offer to repair non-existent faults on people's roofs.

Such practices are absent from primitive societies which still exist in remote regions. However contact with capitalist civilization can quickly corrupt.[1]

Communism has been tried as an alternative to capitalism in the modern world, but so far has been found to bring about its own problems associated with power.

The best counter to corruption and greed is a widespread contact with motivation by intrinsic values. Since every other motivational level is pre-potent to this one, that is a solution which is unlikely to come about.

Moreover it does not help that Maslow's original version of the Hierarchy with self-actualization at the top, is still taught on many psychology and management courses as if it were complete as a theory in spite of having no place for motivation by ethical standards. Instead there is created the false impression that self-actualization is the highest motivation attainable by humans — a view which he later corrected[2] but which has continued to be widely publicised.

CHAPTER 20

Religion

All religions have two major aspects. First is an attempt to explain our origin and that of the world around us together with our relationship to that world. This is about our identity and how we belong. Second is a set of rules and values by which to lead our lives.

The story of the Garden of Eden symbolises these two aspects very well. Adam and Eve were the pinnacle of God's creation and were placed in charge of their environment in a state of innocence like the rest of Nature. But then they became aware of the difference between good and evil, and the nature of shame, by eating the forbidden fruit.

The human species is unique in having a need for intrinsic values, and therefore for a belief in an authority beyond our own personal interests, to be esteemed and worshipped, whether that be God, communism, scientism, or whatever. Karl Marx described religion as 'the opium of the people'[1] and then substituted his own political religion. Richard Dawkins[2] tries to persuade people away from a belief in God in favour of commitment to science.

The danger with these alternatives, as with religion itself, is that at some point some pundit with aspirations of power will dictate what is to be considered acceptable, and there we are with a religion once again.

We cannot get away from this trend in our biological natures. It gives us our noblest aspirations, inspires our finest art, and at the same time has been the basis for our most cruel acts.

Throughout human history wars have been fought on religious grounds and individuals have been slaughtered for believing in something different from their peers. Why are people prepared to die for their beliefs, and why does anyone want to kill those who believe in something different?

To answer these questions we need to examine how it is that a belief becomes entrenched in a person's mind to the point that it must not be challenged. Usually the seeds are implanted in the first few years of a child's life before the age of reason. An infant is reared within a family whose members hold a particular religious or political point of view and the infant perceives the holding of this point of view as normal. By the time he or she is able to reason, such a belief is so taken for granted that it is beyond question. Family ties and the need to belong reinforce the assumed truth and discourage any faint glimmering of doubt.

In this way attitudes get passed on down the generations. The belief becomes a cultural doctrine, and acceptance of that doctrine takes on the aspect of an intrinsic value as well as the ticket which ensures a place within the community to which one belongs.

Of course there are exceptions and sometimes an adult is converted to a new belief. This is like rebirth with new 'parents' and the resulting strength of conviction is, if anything, even stronger. The new faith is reinforced by the conviction that this new viewpoint was arrived at by the use of reason, though this perception of how the conversion came about may be far from the truth.

Any dissenter's arguments threaten the integrity of a community's beliefs and values as well as the associated sense of belonging within that particular culture. So from the community's point of view such persons have to be silenced. But because their convictions are based on faith and not on proof, reason does not come into the equation and the only effective ways to achieve their silence are by imprisonment or by killing them.

Human history's wars fought on religious grounds are legion. Notable were the Crusades, and amongst some Muslim communities the consequent hatred of Christians engendered all those centuries ago can still be inflamed today in support of political objectives.

Then there are all the problems between Jews and Muslims inflamed by the creation of the state of Israel after World War Two, which required the displacement of native Palestinians whose cause was then embraced by Muslims around the world in a spirit of brotherhood and belonging.

Christianity in Europe has a history of bloody struggles between Catholics and Protestants in which political and religious differences went hand in hand. Our own civil war included the beheading of a king and a brief Republic under a Puritan, Oliver Cromwell. Islam appears to be following the same pattern with civil wars in Syria and Libya fuelled by differences between Sunni and Shiite Muslims.

Shared beliefs make people vulnerable to manipulation. Leaders with personal ambitions of power can mobilize their followers to action with rallying cries having a religious significance, as in Northern Ireland where the political struggle was reinforced by linking it with old religious differences. Terrorist leaders, motivated by the lure of power, can justify their cause by persuading their followers that they are upholding God's will and can expect to be rewarded in heaven. Naturally preachers who encourage young men to become suicide bombers do not actually practise what they preach.

The content of what was actually taught by the founders of most of the world's major religions reveals a very different picture. They preached a way of life that would enable their followers to live together in peace and harmony in a stable society, by giving them precepts which were to be accepted as values by which to govern their lives. Those founders would surely be horrified at the ways in which their teachings have been misinterpreted and misused.

The problem has been that those leaders who took over after the founders' deaths lacked their masters' motivations and insights. Instead the lure of power seems to have replaced spiritual integrity. As time went on anyone with a new twist on doctrine could gain respect by adding a fresh myth or precept with the result that eventually the original message became swamped or distorted.

A case in point is that of Jesus' simple message of love and forgiveness which has been overlaid and embroidered by layer upon layer of subsequent legend and doctrine, none of which featured in his teaching as recorded in the gospels. If he were to return today he would be hard pressed to recognize Christianity as the movement which he founded, and the church's history which included the cruelties of witch-hunting and the Inquisition would horrify him.

Sharing a common religion and hence its values can give a community cohesion, but it also puts power in the hands of its leaders who can, and often do, claim divine authority for what is, in fact, their own lust for power. We have plenty of historic examples in the West, some of which were based on the concept of the 'divine right of kings'. Today in the Middle East the self-styled Islamic State commits horrors which they broadcast on the internet, making it plain that their motivation is actually absolute power.

Yet it seems we cannot do without organised religion. Our biologically-rooted need for intrinsic values leads us to seek an authority who can direct our beliefs and proclaim moral and ethical standards by which we can aspire to live our lives. This at least has the advantage of encouraging a shared set of values within any given community, supporting the sense of belonging. Those individuals who make use of religion to boost their own personal power, are motivated by an extreme form of the need for esteem and possibly also a distorted version of self-actualization.

CHAPTER 21

Creativity

The word 'creativity' tends to conjure up an image related to the arts, perhaps Constable painting a landscape, Mozart composing a symphony, or Fonteyn and Nureyev dancing together at the Royal Opera House. The truth is that creativity can be expressed in far more circumstances and situations than these images would suggest.

Creativity is the bringing into being of something that did not exist before, or at least did not exist in the same form. I can think of five different kinds.

1) First there is the transformation of some material object so that its superficial characteristics are changed. We do this when we paint a door, re-organize the furniture in a room, or lay paving stones onto a garden path. Some aspect has been altered compared with what was there before.

2) Next there is the creative urge to use materials in order to produce some completely new object. This can range from rug-making and embroidery to carpentry, metal-work, photography, sculpture and the painting of pictures.

3) The third form of creativity is in the mind. The writer creating a work of fiction, a poet, composer of music, mathematician poring over an abstract problem, scientist bringing forth a new theory to explain physical observations, or an engineer conjuring up a way of solving some constructural problem. But also the day-dreamer simply allowing mental images to come and go.

4) Next we come to performance by a musician, a dancer, an actor. This may be before an audience or it may be enjoyed entirely on one's own in the privacy of home.

5) Finally there is the creation of a baby.

The urge to engage in the first kind of activity is usually to save money. Saving because one is hard up is an attempt to ensure the safety of one's purchasing power for basic necessities. Saving in order to be able to buy an extra item for the home may be to impress visitors in which case we have an expression of the need for esteem, but if it is to give oneself pleasure and satisfaction then it is an expression of one's own individuality, the desire to actualize the self.

The second type of creativity is the occupation of an artisan or artist, and motivation can still be varied. Artists have to eat, so a particular object may be produced purely for the money it can earn when sold. Or it may have been made so that it could be admired along with the kudos of having been its creator. On the other hand this act of creativity may be an outpouring of one's soul, a combination of self-expression and a need to convert into physical form what one values as beautiful or useful. True artists completely lose themselves in the absorption of their task.

Apart from day-dreaming the third type usually involves some motivation to earn one's living, but there tends to be an even stronger urge for recognition and for professional advancement as well as a sense of the value of those ideas which have been produced in terms of their beauty, usefulness, or contribution to the general body of knowledge.

What about day-dreaming? This may be purely the fortuitous result of physical relaxation in a comfortable armchair or it can be a deliberate invocation of one's own creative intuition. Either way images come spontaneously to mind, uninhibited by the chattering of consciousness, and from this flow new ideas can emerge. It can be a valuable technique for inviting inspiration.

The fourth type is artistic performance. For those at the top of their profession the fact of earning money fades into oblivion. All that matters is the quality of their performance as they express their souls in the interpretation of their chosen medium, whether it be dance, music, or drama. Like a painter or sculptor they can completely lose themselves in the activity of creation, so here we have motivation by an intrinsic value.

Finally there is the creation of a baby. Let us assume that it is intentional in which case the motivation is the desire to start or enlarge a family. At a conscious level this is about belonging. At an unconscious level our genes harbour the goal of survival.

Although the five categories of creativity that have been described range from the mundane to the sublime, it has been demonstrated that the drives which motivate each of them do not necessarily follow suit. In fact motivation can be so complicated that it involves several levels of the Hierarchy simultaneously. However whatever other drives may be present every act of creativity is likely to be at least partially motivated by the satisfaction of being able to achieve something new, to actualize some part of oneself, whether it be baking a cake or pouring one's soul into the performance of a concerto.

In my experience transpersonal psychologists have tended to regard creativity as essentially spiritual and therefore motivated at a level beyond self-actualization. It is true that the abstract concept of creativity may be seen as an intrinsic value in its own right, but individual creative acts can result from a wide variety of urges ranging right across the board.

An act of creativity can be the means by which to satisfy any of the needs. But creativity becomes an intrinsic value combined with self-expression when we act solely from the joy of being creative, when the activity is valued purely for its own sake with no thought concerning any advantages to be gained.

CHAPTER 22

Revenge

Revenge is always presented as a desire for justice, 'an eye for an eye and a tooth for a tooth'[1], and is a peculiarly human motivation. We do not find it anywhere else in the animal world where, instead, threat and injury simply trigger the fight or flight response. A rabbit being chased by a fox runs for its life down a burrow, the needs for survival and safety reigning supreme.

When a lion pride's alpha male is killed by a rival, the newcomer also gets rid of all the former's cubs. At first the lionesses attempt to protect their off-spring but soon accept the inevitable situation and succumb to the new regime. There is no evidence that they ever try to get their own back in a spirit of revenge against the new alpha male.

The specifically human nature of a desire for revenge is consistent with being in the category of an intrinsic value since the Hierarchy is based on the evolutionary development of species and motivation by intrinsic values seems to appear only among humans.[2] It is related to a sense of justice.

Turning the other cheek does not come naturally to our species. Cultures which condemn taking revenge into one's own hands, substitute a system of laws and punishments in order to maintain order, so that the state punishes miscreants on behalf of those whom they have caused to suffer. When justice is applied effectively victims are able to feel they have satisfied their vengeance vicariously, and frequently that is actually what is meant by the modern euphemism 'achieving closure' when applied to court cases.

The problem with revenge is that it snowballs. A offends B, so B takes it out on A. A is now the victim and retaliates towards B, and so it goes on. Their families and wider communities might get involved, instigating vendettas to which there is no end, carrying the motive for retribution down through succeeding generations. To name just two examples, the enmity felt even today by some Muslims towards

Christians had its origins in the Crusades nine centuries ago, and ancient ethnic rivalries in Serbia resulted in massacres at the end of the twentieth century.

Arguably the most famous fictional story which deals with this form of enmity is Romeo and Juliet. There is no surprise in the fact that Shakespeare presented it in the style of a tragedy with a moral lesson.

In fact his plays are full of examples in which the characters are motivated by a desire for revenge. Take 'The Merchant of Venice'. Here Shylock conceives a plan to demand a pound of flesh in retribution for all the insults and indignities he had suffered because of his race. His chosen victim is a representative of all those perceived to have been responsible.

On a lighter note in 'A Midsummer's Night's Dream' Oberon, king of the fairies, gets his henchman Puck to play a trick on Titania in retaliation for refusing a request. In a comedy everything ends happily but this is not always the case in real life. People who play tricks on others usually end up the butt of someone else's joke. This is known as 'getting one's own back' or 'teaching the other a lesson'.

Teaching the other side a lesson can, of course, be more violent. It is often the motive behind gang killings when the honour of one gang and the pride of its leader are seen to have been violated.

The destructiveness of revenge was recognised in antiquity at least as far back in history as Moses the law-giver who forbade it on the grounds that it attempted to usurp the authority of God: 'Vengeance is mine, saith the Lord'[3]. Jesus went even further with 'Love your enemies'[4], and Buddha advocated moderation and restraint, the Middle Way. But do we listen? No, the urge to retaliate takes over. We get this fixed idea in our heads that a person or group must be taught a lesson they will never forget. Prejudice is an attitude while revenge is action, both coming from the same source within us, a capacity for hatred linked to supposed justification. Historic examples are legion: Protestant v Catholic, Sunni v Shia, ethnic cleansing, and all forms of hate crime.

In relation to the Hierarchy the hurt that is avenged can be on any one of the seven levels of need. The compulsion to exact revenge generation after generation is fuelled by hatred of the intended family, class or race, a negative on the level of belonging which defines our identity in terms of 'us and them'. If pride has been violated then the motivation is wounded self- esteem, for example road rage and probably most drunken brawls.

However vengeance as a pure concept is on the dark side of intrinsic values since it is negatively related to honour, justice and fairness. Naturally it is not perceived as a negative by those who embrace it as an imperative to restore their own damaged honour. Values opposed to vengeance include humility, forgiveness and compassion.

CHAPTER 23

The Shadow

Have you ever experienced a sense of shock when someone you know well behaves completely out of character? What on earth has come over them?!! Polite Pam suddenly loses her temper and rails at everyone present. Bold Bernard chickens out of an activity with his friends. Pious Prudence has an affair with a married man. Examples are endless.

Some of these behaviours may be the result of an earlier trauma such as those described in the chapter on Childhood, the reaction being the result of association, but they may also be the person's Shadow rearing its head.

The Shadow can be defined briefly as that function of an individual's unconscious which is the repository for all the suppressed parts of his or her psychological make-up.[1]

At birth Nature has already determined certain of our characteristics through the genes and conditions in the womb, but Nurture still has its role to play. Life in the womb and the shock of being born have had their effect, but our psyches are still relatively undetermined and await the formative lessons of life. At this stage we are capable of anything, of developing almost any possible characteristic, almost any imaginable personality. We have the potential to become a saint or a sinner, criminal or law-abiding, respectful or iconoclastic, determined or wavering, sociable or a loner, independent or clinging — and more. The future is as yet unwritten. The adult to be is still mainly a blank slate and depends largely on the lessons yet to be learned in childhood.

The social aspects of a child's learning process are about those behaviours and attitudes to avoid, usually because they cause negative experiences in the physiological, belonging or esteem needs. These are then banished into the unconscious and become parts of what is known as the Shadow. This is a natural process driven by our needs in the Hierarchy, and every one of us has a Shadow. The chapter on Childhood has already given some indication of how it comes about. Without this learning process of socialisation anarchy would reign.

In order to be able to fit into society children have to learn about relating to others, and how to distinguish between those behaviours which are acceptable and those which are not. Mainly this task falls to parents and teachers, but what they teach depends on their own individual outlooks. One little boy is taught to stand up for himself and is praised if he inflicts upon another child a well-earned lesson, while another lad is taught to avoid fights because they solve nothing and only snowball into more animosity.

Children also learn by imitation. Inevitably they copy parental behaviour and try it out with their friends. Any time one comes across a five-year-old behaving like an adult, it may be amusing to observe but it also reveals much about one or another parent.

One little girl is taught to be ladylike and polite while rudeness and plain-speaking are relegated to the Shadow because they elicit disapproval and are a threat to belonging and esteem. On the other hand another little girl copies her mother who is outspoken and speaks her mind regardless of whose feelings she tramples upon and in this manner gets her own way, so in this case it is politeness and consideration for others' feelings that find their way into the child's unconscious alter ego as weaknesses.

Then there are the lessons learned by direct experience. A clever child creates envy and finds that he is not liked, so he plays down his intellect by banishing seriousness and becoming a bit of a clown.

The characteristics which are suppressed are those which the individual perceives as deleterious to one of his or her seven hierarchical needs. However such judgments are not universal and what one person sees as a threat may actually be embraced by another. One child suppresses rebelliousness, another conformity. One suppresses adventurousness, another timidity.

Thus we learn which behaviours and attitudes are advantageous and which are bad and to be avoided. The latter are then suppressed. The potential represented by the latter is shunned and relegated to the unconscious, leaving only its opposite for future self-expression. People then come to believe that the suppressed undesirable characteristics were never a part of their potential at all. Complete denial ensues.

When we encounter in others those same characteristics which we have suppressed in ourselves, usually we condemn them as bad but just occasionally we admire and envy them as something of which we are incapable.

In time a complete picture of the person's character and personality is formed out of those behaviours which were allowed to remain after the denial of their opposites. The down side of this learning process is that most of the time we are left with only half of our potential, and it is only in explosive and uncontrollable outbursts that the other half emerges.

The suppressed characteristics have not gone away. Far from it. They are stored at an unconscious level. It is as if there is an opposite person lurking in one's psyche, having all the features that one regards as undesirable or reprehensible. They can reappear in nightmares, usually in the form of a dark figure.

Occasionally some occurrence will trigger an aspect of the Shadow to come to the surface and express itself, resulting in behaviour of which the unfortunate individual can only say 'I don't know what came over me. I would never do a thing like that.' Someone who is normally subdued suddenly lets fly at another, while on the other hand someone who is normally domineering reacts to another with weakness. A person who prides himself on always being truthful, tells a lie. A hardened criminal performs an act of kindness — but is careful to keep it secret from his fellows! A religious person suddenly has doubts. A disciplinarian takes to drinking excessively.

If the emergence of the Shadow becomes a serious problem psychotherapy may be able to help. The idea is to re-integrate the two opposing halves, that which is conscious and that which was suppressed, thereby making the whole spectrum of responses available once again. Hopefully the individual will then be able to choose the appropriate response in all relevant situations.

As a child Hildegarde was outspoken as are most small children. But at age thirteen she began expressing radical opinions about religion and politics which caused her schoolmates to view her with suspicion, so she turned into a quiet and reticent teenager and adult. She regarded herself as being considerate of other people's feelings by not expressing her own controversial views and never criticising anyone else's point of view. She was completely unaware that she had actually suppressed her own ability to speak out.

In her thirties she trained as a therapist, and one particular workshop session was designed to enable the students to cope with difficult and aggressive clients. It involved working in pairs, taking it in turns to hurl at one's partner whatever provocative attitude one could muster, with the safety caveat of no touching.

When it became Hildegarde's turn to be the provocateur something inside her surfaced. She really got into her stride and let it rip. The teacher had the good sense to allow this to continue, having observed that Hildegarde's partner was coping well. At the end of the exercise she said to Hildegarde 'You enjoyed that, didn't you?' to which the amazed reply was a definite 'yes'.

From that moment on Hildegarde's ability to speak out was restored. She had got in touch with that particular aspect of her Shadow and had accepted it back into her consciousness, so that she was now able to respond to situations with access to the full range of responses from fearless self-expression to keeping her peace, whichever was most appropriate.

Before leaving the Shadow mention must be made of LSD which temporarily weakens the barrier keeping suppressed material at bay in the unconscious. This was why it was originally thought to have potential for being useful in psychotherapy.[2] However the full force of the confrontation with aspects of one's own psyche which one regards as shameful or embarrassing can be truly terrifying. A shy person can suddenly be confronted with their own aggression, a bold person with their own cowardice, a leader with weakness and frailty. Thankfully the majority of trips in the 1960's apparently did not plumb those depths but the few that did were instrumental in leading to its sale and use being declared illegal.

CHAPTER 24

Self-Interest

The word 'self-interest' is often used pejoratively, but this is misleading and does us a disservice. Six of our seven categories of motivation are in the service of the self and are natural to our species, having developed as a product of the evolutionary process. If we were not so motivated then we would not be being fully human, just as a captive leopard that does not hunt for food is not being fully a leopard.

Of course each of us puts our own survival above all else. Of course we have to eat and drink. Naturally we seek a social life with congenial relationships, and as good a life-style as possible.

Provided we are also in touch with the positive aspect of the seventh category then all these self-interests will be pursued as far as possible in a manner which is not harmful to oneself or to others. However every one of the first six needs is pre-potent to intrinsic values, so we should not be surprised at behaviour which appears to be selfish. It is natural and normal to look after number one.

It is this same proclivity for self-interested motivation on which advertisers rely when trying to persuade us how much better off we should be by purchasing their particular product, or politicians when conducting an election campaign.

Many a citizen has sent a complaint or a suspicion of malpractice to a government department or the head of an organization, only to receive a reply which either attempts to explain away the issue or completely misunderstands the problem. It is only those who are prepared to keep on badgering and in some cases willing to conduct a lengthy campaign, that find the matter is eventually investigated properly.

Do all bureaucrats require their staff to be trained in the gentle art of fobbing people off? Why is this such a common experience? The answer is simple. All these bodies and organizations are run by human beings, each of whom has his or her own outlook on life, personality, hang-ups and motivations. No manager wants his department to become branded as inefficient or worse, and many will discourage their staff from admitting to a fault in the system. There is a closing of ranks along with an attempt to cover-up. Complainants are sent a standard reply along the lines: 'We operate to the highest standards. If any irregularities are discovered then lessons will be learned.'

Employees who do not wish to fall foul of their boss will go along with any whitewash, and those who leak revelations because their sense of ethical behaviour is violated (intrinsic values) risk retribution. Threats of dismissal are effective in silencing most would-be whistle-blowers because the loss of one's job without a reference will make finding another difficult and will bring hardship to one's family as well as scuppering career prospects. All of these considerations are pre-potent to values and it is only those individuals who feel their outrage most strongly who will not succumb to the threats.

In any organization corruption comes from the top. If it is just an individual employee who is at fault, then as soon as this is discovered that person is dealt with and probably dismissed. But if the boss is guilty of malpractice then this seeps down the entire system because he/she employs only those people who can be trusted to go along with corrupt methods and attitudes and not land the boss in trouble.

A well publicised recent example is that of phone hacking by news-paper journalists in order to obtain exclusive, and sometimes sensa-tional, stories. This practice is illegal so, of course, they kept quiet about the method employed. When the practice was first revealed it was assumed to be the work of just one rogue individual reporter whose methods were unknown either to his superiors or to his colleagues. However as more and more evidence came to light it became clear that phone hacking was endemic within the newspaper organization which employed him.

Revelations from the last fifty years or so have uncovered con-cealment by the Catholic Church of paedophilia by some of their own priests. The perpetrators were simply moved to a different location where they could carry on their practices anew. Effectively this was a cover-up. Moreover what does one expect of men who are required to be celibate, denying a basic natural physiological need?

Exposure of corruption requires an outsider who is able to collect robust evidence. Investigative journalists are in the forefront of this enterprise by posing as prospective employees or clients while operating concealed cameras. Television documentaries have exposed all kinds of malpractice, including cruel or uncaring treatment of vulnerable patients in care homes, poor conditions in a detention centre, bogus colleges enrolling fake students so they can enter this country, and all sorts of illegal situations too numerous to mention.

When the nations of the world get together at international conferences to discuss climate change and dwindling resources, they all know what is at stake but each country is out to defend its own interests. Rich nations want to keep their living standards while poor ones want to better themselves in order to live like the others. These representatives are mostly educated people and know the dangers and what needs to be done, but their priorities appear to be the immediate short-term interests of their own people, their standing within their own political parties, and whether they are likely to retain power at the next election. Long-term issues receive little effective consideration. They would justify this stance by using two arguments: they are there to serve their own peoples' wishes, and in order to be able to do some good they have to stay in office next time round. If they do happen to achieve some miniscule step forward in spite of this attitude then credit is claimed for upholding values against stiff opposition.

All of this should not surprise us. Of the seven motivation levels in the Hierarchy it is only the one at the top, intrinsic values, which is not about looking after number one. Certainly we can act altruistically, in other words at this seventh level of the Hierarchy, but in any given situation it is a mistake to assume that this will be the case unless there are good grounds for the assumption. And it is vital to remember that, whatever the organization or situation, it involves human individuals for whom all six levels of self-interested motivation are pre-potent to altruism.

We are not ants or termites, programmed to act for the common good. Those creatures belong to a totally different branch of the evolutionary tree. 'The selfish gene' is an apt description of our biological inheritance and therefore of our customary reactions.

Nevertheless we have evolved that extra motivation, namely the urge to pursue a value, to transcend our baser instincts. It is just that the other levels are pre-potent to this one so it takes priority only when felt very strongly.

CHAPTER 25

Know Thyself

The system which has been presented in Part 1 is complete and is a continuum. It is complete in the sense that it covers all possible human motivations ranging from the physical through the emotional and social to the spiritual. It is a continuum in that all parts of it are inter-related in a seamless manner with no gaps. It is a product of that other continuum, the evolutionary process.

Maslow was a victim of his own success. His first version of the Hierarchy of Needs which was published in 1943, was an instant hit in spite of his acknowledgement that it was incomplete, and it was widely accepted. The later additional level, intrinsic values, appeared in a journal which was relatively obscure at that time and went largely unnoticed, with the result that his earlier incomplete version continues to be reproduced today in countless publications and courses.

It is hoped that all future publications of Maslow's Hierarchy will include this extra level as he clearly intended. All other levels of motivation involve self-interest, whether it be looking after one's own health and well-being, relationships, social standing or career and opportunities. Without intrinsic values this is a theory that has no place for ethics, philanthropy, aesthetics or religious beliefs, whereas clearly these play important roles in human motivation.

Moreover we share most of our motivating drives with other creatures — food, shelter, safety, procreation, family relationships, even including the need to be fully who, or what, we are. It is only our sense of morals and ability to appreciate the finer things of life, in other words our spiritual aspect, that defines our humanity and lifts us above the level of other species. Without these characteristics we are no more human than a chimpanzee — just a bit more clever, that is all.

Human motivation is complex with an abundant variety of possible triggers. Nevertheless whatever be a person's driving forces they can always be assigned to one or another of the seven categories. The

Motivation Hierarchy is a complete system and would not be so if any one of the seven were missing.

In our best novels and plays, just as in real life, the plot arises directly from the characters and their motives without having to have recourse to coincidence and happenstance. Shakespeare's tragedies are prime examples. The fate of Macbeth is sealed when his wife succumbs to the lure of power and he surrenders to her persuasion. The fate of Romeo and Juliet is a foregone conclusion, one way or another, given the feud between their rival families.

The same can be said of the best who-dunnits. Agatha Christie and Dorothy Sayers rely for the resolution of their mysteries on motivation which is in character.

The early Christian church had its own method for codifying motivations which led to sin. The Penguin Encyclopedia defines the Seven Deadly Sins as follows: 'The fundamental vices thought, in the Christian tradition, to underlie all sinful actions. They are pride, covetousness, lust, envy, gluttony, anger, sloth.' [1]

...and so woman gets the blame for everything

(THE ORIGINAL SIN)

What is remarkable is that this list from centuries ago fits neatly into the dark side of the Motivation Hierarchy. Gluttony and sloth are negative motives at the physiological level, lust has elements of both physiological and belonging needs, pride (in its negative connotation) and envy are aspects of the esteem need with covetousness at belonging and self-actualization. Anger can be thought of as a negation of belonging and arises from a negative experience on any one of the levels. The doctrine of Seven Deadly Sins itself constitutes a belief which belongs with intrinsic values.

In each of us there lurks a Shadow, waiting to be triggered but without our having the slightest inkling of its existence. This aspect of our being cannot be destroyed and any attempt to suppress it will only make it even stronger. Understanding it in order to integrate it into consciousness is the best solution.

The whole gamut of motives stem from the very first biological imperative, to survive. Humans have become so successful in this respect that we are now swamping the planet with over-population, threatening the survival of other species and ultimately of life itself — except perhaps the life of bacteria which are keeping abreast of our attacks by reinventing themselves.

There are those who warn the world to take note and change but so far they are in a minority. It is likely that we shall end up with such severe shortages in water, food, energy and living space, that the outcome will be a proliferation of wars of increasing destructive power which will eventually devastate the planet.

Religion could buck this trend since it is supposed to be about values and is supported by its own authority. It really is time that the various religions dropped their doctrinal squabbles and took responsibility for saving humanity and preserving that life on Earth which they teach was of divine creation. This task cannot just be left to the scientific community whose voice has not the same influence as that of religious pronouncement.

In order to be better adjusted and therefore happier in life, it helps if we understand ourselves and those forces which tend to produce our own actions and attitudes. It also helps if we can understand where those people are coming from with whom we have to interact. This applies not just to communication between individuals but also to relationships in the international arena.

An ancient maxim was 'Know thyself', and indeed the world would be a much better place if self-knowledge were the norm.

PART 2:

STEP BY STEP

CHAPTER 26

How Did That Happen?

Have you ever had a conversation with someone which seemed to be perfectly normal, and which suddenly descended into an argument for no apparent reason? Have you ever had to deal with someone who could be described as 'difficult'? Over and over again there are unintended outcomes when humans interact with each other and one wonders: 'How on earth did that happen?'

The answer could be that there was a simple misunderstanding in which case good communication should sort it out. But frequently the cause is more complicated. Being able to handle people in a tricky situation requires sensitivity, perception and skill. To some this ability seems to come naturally whereas others have a knack for putting their foot in it and only manage to make matters worse. There are those who can encounter an explosive confrontation and calm it down with their instinctive understanding of the human psyche. There are also manipulators who can use this same ability to twist people round their own little fingers and gain some advantage.

What is this knowledge they possess? Can it be codified and transmitted to the rest of us? The following pages are an attempt to do just that. Hopefully this knowledge will enable the reader to guard against those who would use it for their own selfish ends.

The Scale of Responses was designed in the late 1960's by a Jungian psychiatrist, Ian Marshall[1], as part of a complete psychotherapeutic system which he called Sequential Analysis[2]. In 1967-1970 he trained a few psychotherapists, including myself, in his techniques but unfortunately although our paper on the Scale appeared in an academic journal in 1997[3] he never published the complete system.

However the Scale is worth publishing on its own because it is applicable to a much wider context than the consulting room. It can be used by any one of us in everyday life. Everyone can benefit. It can help us understand others better and enable us to recognise our own habitual attitudes and responses. This way we have the ability to gain some degree of mastery over our spontaneous reactions instead of being their slaves. That has to be a good thing.

The responses covered by the Scale range from the personal, through the interpersonal, to the spiritual or transpersonal. They are connected by patterns and form a complete and seamless continuum, covering all possible responses.

CHAPTER 27

The Scale of Responses

CHART 1

The Scale of Responses
as a ladder

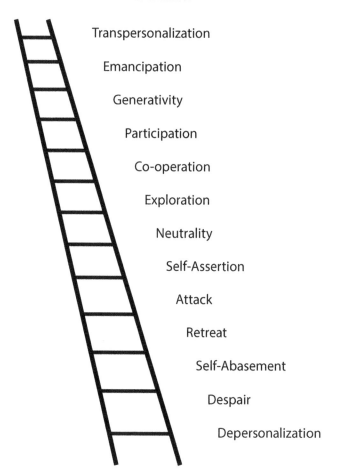

Transpersonalization

Emancipation

Generativity

Participation

Co-operation

Exploration

Neutrality

Self-Assertion

Attack

Retreat

Self-Abasement

Despair

Depersonalization

The word 'responses' will be used to cover all kinds of reactions to situations, whether they be changes in emotion or attitude, and whether they be experienced internally or outwardly expressed. For example on hearing her child cry a mother becomes alerted and rushes to offer comfort, and on being insulted one man would respond with fisticuffs while another feels resentment but remains silent. Responses can be active or passive, outwardly expressed or just inwardly felt.

The Scale of Responses consists of thirteen items each of which covers a broad category, and taken together they comprise the whole spectrum of possible moods and reactions that humans can experience.

The Scale's thirteen items are arranged in a specific order (Chart 1 - on the previous page). It can be compared to a ladder ascending from hell to heaven. Like a step-ladder it is then folded in half (Chart 2 - opposite) which reveals a pattern of six pairs of opposites. It is this latter chart which is crucial to an understanding of the following pages, and the reader might wish to copy it onto a separate piece of paper for ease of reference.

Each pair bears a positive and a negative sign. *Those on the right which are labelled with a plus sign, are all responses in which the individual has some degree of acceptance of the situation, whereas the minus items are those in which to some degree one wants the situation to be different.* It is not intended that plus/minus should be interpreted as value judgments implying that those responses are good/bad.

What is much more relevant is whether a response is appropriate in a given situation. It is appropriate to feel remorse (-4:Self-Abasement) if one's actions have caused harm, and to be angry (-2:Attack) in the face of cruelty or injustice, even though these responses carry a minus sign. Any reaction on the plus side in these circumstances would be regarded as inappropriate to say the least. It is inappropriate to aid and abet (+2:Co-operation) someone engaged in torture or terrorism, and a response on the minus side would be expected as appropriate.

'Anyone can become angry — that is easy. But to be angry with the right person, to the right degree, at the right time, for the right purpose, and in the right way — this is not easy.'
Aristotle, The Nichomachean Ethics

The principle of appropriate response is so universally understood that people pretend to regret the passing of someone they disliked, apologise when they have caused offence even though they meant every word they said, and congratulate their successful opponents in spite of resentment that they have been robbed of coveted trophies.

CHART 2

The Scale of Responses
showing pairs of opposites

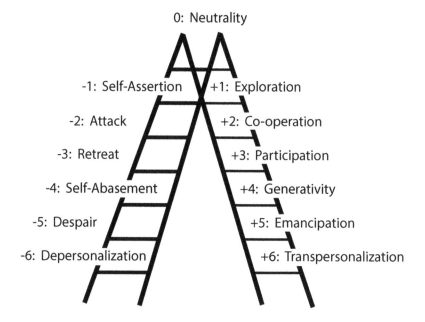

0: Neutrality

-1: Self-Assertion	+1: Exploration
-2: Attack	+2: Co-operation
-3: Retreat	+3: Participation
-4: Self-Abasement	+4: Generativity
-5: Despair	+5: Emancipation
-6: Depersonalization	+6: Transpersonalization

Apart from 0 each response can be either active or passive.

In Britain there is currently a trend for demanding public apologies whenever a government official or a company director gets things wrong, when we all know that the use of apologetic phrases is no guarantee that the appropriate feeling is attached to such a declaration.   Unlike the culture in Japan we do not give importance to face-saving.   Immediate remedial action and compensation would be far more convincing.

Chart 3 describes the principles which underlie the six pairs of opposites, ranging from the relationship of the self to the situation which is found at ± 1, through the social bands, to the spiritual at ± 5 and ± 6. These pairs together with 0:Neutrality, form the basis for the seven chapters which follow.

As Part 2 is all about the interpretation and application of the Scale of Responses the reader is advised to make a loose-leaf copy of Charts 2 and 3 for ease of reference.

CHART 3
Opposites

±1: establishing the nature of a situation

±2: functioning with, or against, others

±3: totally involved in,
        or withdrawn from, the situation

±4: feeling extremes of capability

±5: extremes of the spirit

±6: ego-less states

The symbol ± is used to mean '+ or −'. Plus indicates some degree of acceptance, and minus some degree of non-acceptance of the situation.

The reader might wish to copy Charts 2 and 3
onto a separate piece of paper for convenience of reference
when examples are discussed.

CHAPTER 28

Neutrality

At the top of Chart 2 is Neutrality which has been assigned the number 0. This indicates no reaction at all, which might be because nothing in particular is happening or because what is occurring has no effect.

This is not the same as deliberately ignoring something. An example of Neutrality would be a person taking a lie detector test, not at all worried by the situation, sitting comfortably, not thinking about anything in particular, and nothing registers on the apparatus.

Another example is that moment of hesitation following examination of a new situation and before deciding what to do about it. This is quite different from an attempt to conceal guilt by not reacting, or failure to greet an acquaintance out of shyness, or ignoring a troublemaker, all of which are definable responses.

Neutrality differs from boredom which involves a wish for things to be different from how they are and which thereby satisfies the criterion for being allocated to the minus side of the Scale. It is also not the same as non-resistance, going with the flow, as that involves some degree of acceptance of the situation which is the criterion for a response on the plus side. Neutrality stands between plus and minus.

This is a relaxed state since it is neither for nor against anything but is not the same as the relaxed state produced by meditation. The latter belongs higher up the Scale in +5 or +6 and will be considered later. The difference lies in the fact that at Neutrality consciousness is normal, there is a clear sense of self and of one's own identity, and there is no purpose, whereas in meditation there is an underlying aim to transcend the self and enter an altered state of consciousness.

In Neutrality there is no intention to detach from the cares of everyday life and in fact there is no intention at all. There is not even an intention to do nothing.

Neutrality is also not the same as being asleep which is an altered state of consciousness.

In my childhood I was a veritable bookworm, my eyes frequently focussed on a book. If my mother called to me I was so engrossed I literally did not hear. She had to call more loudly in order to gain my attention. When reading I was probably in +3:Participation, identifying with the characters in the story and empathising with them, possibly even experiencing their reactions vicariously. But from my mother's point of view I had offered no reaction at all. She perceived me as being in 0:Neutrality and responded accordingly.

People's reactions are to their perception of the other's attitude which is not necessarily a true reflection of what is actually going on in the other person's psyche. It happens frequently that silence is incorrectly interpreted as an attitude of being unaffected, of not caring, in fact of Neutrality, when it could be due to a host of other possibilities. The incorrect assumption may then give rise to a whole scenario of interactions, all of which could have been avoided had the absence of response been correctly interpreted.

It may seem odd to include Neutrality on the chart at all. However as we delve more deeply into possible reactions it will be seen that this zero position does actually have a role to play in the overall scheme of things. It is necessary to have a zero position on the Scale in order to represent no response even though this is often just an incorrect assumption on the part of a second individual.

So for the time being the reader is asked to accept the inclusion of 0: Neutrality as a kind of response, albeit one with zero content. This is comparable to describing a car that is at rest as having a speed which happens to be 0 miles per hour.

CHAPTER 29

Self-Assertion and Exploration

Self-Assertion and Exploration, which have been assigned the numbers -1 and +1, are to do with establishing the nature of a situation. In Exploration we look outwards, seeking to discover or understand what is going on, whereas in Self-Assertion we aim to impose on the situation our own view of how things should be. For example a teacher says to her pupils: 'Now turn to page 10.' She is in -1: Self-Assertion, giving an instruction simply and non-aggressively, and probably assumes or hopes that the pupils will comply by opening their books in a spirit of +1: Exploration.

The plus sign does not necessarily imply that Exploration is a good thing. Take, for example, the nosey parker trying to find out salacious gossip. Equally the minus sign does not necessarily imply that Self-Assertion is undesirable. The teacher has to control her class, the foreman has to give orders to his team, and the sergeant expects obedience from his soldiers.

The ability to command is as much a matter of personal attitude and expectations as it is of actual actions. So many people in positions of authority get this wrong. They shout and bully as if this

is the only way to demonstrate their power. They mistake -2:Attack for -1:Self-Assertion. True authority is reasonable, calm and controlled. It expects instructions to be followed and therefore has no need to resort to any form of intimidation. These are the qualities that define a true leader.

By contrast in +1:Exploration people simply observe without endeavouring to impose their own will. Thus the ideal scientist dispassionately observes an experiment

without any wish for it to go one way or another. A naturalist explores the environment and its creatures without in any way wishing to change them. A student poring over something new tries to absorb its contents.

The criterion for including a response on the plus side of the Scale is that it entails some degree of acceptance of the situation, and in the three examples just described that is the case. They involve a desire to find out what is there without in any way contaminating the evidence or the content.

Here also we have an interviewer endeavouring to obtain information. I mean, of course, the ideal member of that profession and not one of those confrontational interviewers we sometimes find on television news programmes, who persistently interrupt their subjects in order to express an alternative point of view and drown out what the interviewee wanted to say. They think they are eliciting information by being provocative, but in fact they only annoy and may obscure information by imposing their own take on the situation. That is -1:Self-Assertion masquerading as +1:Exploration.

Self-Assertion includes striving to win, so here we find competition, as in school sports, provided there is no animosity and aggression in which case the activity would be in -2:Attack.

Here in Self-Assertion are people who believe they are right in their opinions, including bigots and the prejudiced. That is until they become antagonistic in which case they, too, have gone into -2:Attack.

Impatience and boredom may also be found as features of Self-Assertion. They both involve a desire for the situation to be different, which places them on the minus side of the Scale, and they are both ways in which we assert to ourselves that we are in discomfort and want out.

Exploration is attentive and receptive, tolerant and fair, while Self-Assertion will ignore and insist and may experience impatience to ensure that wishes are put into effect. But in neither of these two is a relationship involved. There is a separation between observer and observed, agent and object. As soon as there is some kind of personal involvement with the object of our attention we are into the next pair.

CHAPTER 30

Attack and Co-operation

This pair, +2:Co-operation and -2:Attack, are about functioning with, or against, others. A family who live together have to co-operate frequently to keep the peace. If they eat together then they have to agree on mealtimes. Most importantly they need to co-operate on the use of the one and only bathroom first thing in the morning when getting ready to go to work and school, and in the evening they need to agree about which programme to watch on the one and only TV set. When Co-operation fails Attack may be the result in the form of arguments or resentment.

Attack does not just cover physical assault. It includes all kinds of feelings of opposition whether openly manifested or quietly simmering inside, such as, for example, envy and harbouring a grievance.

Serving soldiers are acting within this pair for at least some of their time. They co-operate with their colleagues and attack the enemy.

The same can be said about those who engage in team sports. These activities are encouraged in schools precisely because they develop a sense of co-operation, of taking part, of doing one's bit. Each player has his or her position on the field and is not expected to encroach on the role of a team-mate, and there are agreed rules and conventions to be observed.

Team sports also contain a competitive element at -1:Self-Assertion, but this can degenerate into animosity and aggression against the opposing team, in other words -2:Attack. This is not necessarily a bad thing if it simply results in determination to win, but any infringement of the rules calls for a penalty. Unfortunately their supporters are not so regulated as evidenced by pub brawls later in the day.

The antagonistic component at -2:Attack which distinguishes it from competition in -1:Self-Assertion can also be seen in business settings. At a committee or board meeting hopefully there is a general atmosphere of +2:Co-operation, give and take, but in order to achieve

anything it is necessary to have members who are prepared to go into
-1:Self-Assertion mode to make their point. However if failing to
obtain agreement they may feel that other members are hostile and so
they go into a mood of -2:Attack, either openly expressed or just felt.
They may accuse their colleagues of self-serving motives, failure to
understand the issues, and even of illegal practices. Or they may just
silently envy and begrudge the influence that another member wields.

The transition from -1:Self-Assertion to -2:Attack can be explosive
as when suddenly losing one's temper on not getting what was wanted,
or it can be subtle as in the progression from expressing a point of view
to feeling critical of an opponent.

In elections this pair -2:Attack and +2:Co-operation come to the
fore. Party members support and express praise for their own candidate
while decrying the opponent's policies. During campaigns for election
of a party leader there are praise and admiration for one candidate and
disparagement of the other, while a candidate may well feel envy of the
other's popularity.

There is no suggestion that plus and minus have implications of
good and bad, right and wrong. What matters is whether a response is
appropriate and will lead to a satisfactory result. After all, -2:Attack
could be in defence of a vulnerable victim and would be regarded as the
right response. Conversely +2:Co-operation could be with a criminal in
what the law dubs 'aiding and abetting' and would be judged as wrong-
ful action in spite of being allocated a + sign on the chart.

Just as with all the other items this pair can be passive or active,
quietly felt or outwardly expressed. Attack can be silent fuming or
an assault, protest or silent resentment, and Co-operation might be

unexpressed approval or active consideration and assistance. We cannot always judge a person's response simply by observing their actions.

Someone harbouring a grudge is in a mood of Attack even though there is no physical or verbal assault. Someone who quietly admires or is grateful to another is in a mood of Co-operation by the very fact that there is an approving attitude towards the other, even though there may be no overt act to corroborate that inner feeling.

CHAPTER 31

Retreat and Participation

Next we come to -3:Retreat and +3:Participation. Participation is deeper than +2:Co-operation. It describes the degree to which one's whole being is involved in the ongoing activity, situation or relationship.

Someone thoroughly enjoying a swinging party is in this response. The members of a band who get on well together are usually at this level when practising or engaged in a performance. The competent actor on stage who identifies with his character regardless of whether it is a villain or a saint, is in +3:Participation, in contrast to a child who is expected to act in the school play and takes part in a spirit of +2:Co-operation simply because that is what he has been told to do.

When in Participation there is a sense of identification with the group or the activity rather than just taking part. At this level we find trust and empathy as well as honesty and intimacy. While +2:Co-operation is characterised by agreement, +3:Participation is about bonding. Whereas Co-operation is about taking part, joining in, following the rules, Participation goes further. People are totally involved in their activity and there is a bonding between those taking part.

Consider the pensioner who invites her friend round for a cup of tea. The latter Co-operates by arriving at the agreed time, and meanwhile the former has been preparing the tea things also in a spirit of Co-operation. By the time they sit down and get chatting about reminiscences and gossip they become involved with each other and are now in Participation.

-3:Retreat is the natural opposite to Participation since it implies a complete absence of involvement. This is the shy person who sits out at a party, the one who 'switches off' mentally when in undesirable company, or the person who walks away from a dangerous confrontation. It is someone in pain or sorrow and therefore temporarily disconnected from everyday matters. It includes suspiciousness of another as well as attempting to hide a secret, for the very act of concealment means that one is disengaged from the other person — a barrier has been erected. Here also we find someone who does not trust or does not care.

While -2:Attack refuses to accept the given situation and desires to effect some change, -3:Retreat withdraws from contact with whatever is ongoing instead of considering how to do something about it. The former aims to change the situation itself in some way while the latter distances oneself from the situation, or attempts to do so as in the case of physical pain of the kind which causes us to cringe.

Distortion of reality lies behind attitudes of theatricality and coquetry, so these too are allocated to -3:Retreat.

Retreat should not be confused with 0:Neutrality which also describes a form of absence. The difference is that Retreat is an actual

response elicited by the situation, whereas in Neutrality we are simply unaffected by whatever is going on. On a lie-detector Neutrality produces no changes at all whereas Retreat sends the skin resistance soaring up.[1]

In this pair, Participation and Retreat, one is totally involved or totally uninvolved in the ongoing situation.

This might seem to suggest that a gang fight in which adrenalin levels are high is an example of +3:Participation, but that is not usually the case. Although there may be an element of participation in relation to fellow members of the same gang, the mood actually being experienced by each participant is one of aggression against the other gang which locates them in -2:Attack.[2]

However if eventually one side is defeated then members of the losing gang may well go into -3:Retreat as they either run away or suffer pain from their wounds.

CHAPTER 32

Self-Abasement and Generativity

+4:Generativity and -4:Self-Abasement are the pair which relate to the conviction we have concerning our ability to deal with what we can or cannot change or achieve. They are about success and failure, from the self-confidence that is ready for anything that life can throw up, to the feeling of worthlessness and helplessness that we can do nothing to change things. These are the two extremes of the sense of power to effect change.

On the plus side Generativity is a state of being in which we are on top of all the tasks that present themselves, and there is a feeling of confidence, of having the capability to tackle any situation. There is a sense of joy and enthusiasm. So a person who is committed to his task and raring to go is at this level on the Scale.

In a normal loving family a child will tend to perceive his parents as being in Generativity, able to do anything that is needed, even if in reality they are somewhere quite different on the chart. From the child's point of view it is they who put food on the table, can mend any broken

toy and cure a sore throat, and are ready to give guidance for tackling something new.

While +4:Generativity has a joyful and creative approach to dealing with eventualities, -4:Self-Abasement feels inadequate, burdened by situations with which we cannot cope, with a sense of inability to reverse the situation in which we find ourselves. The individual who has been unemployed for some time may reach the conclusion that he will never get a job because he is not good enough, or the jilted lover feel that his rejection is somehow his own fault. Typical statements at this level are: 'I am no good', 'I cannot cope',

'It is all my fault', 'There is nothing I can do'.

Feelings of unworthiness and of guilt and shame are found here, and also, perhaps surprisingly, grief, loss and disappointment, due to the fact that one is genuinely unable to reverse the situation however much one may wish this to be possible. It is also quite common for close friends and relatives of a recently deceased person, to blame themselves for not having done more for that individual while still alive and now it is too late.

Home-sickness is another feature of this level on the Scale. There is a longing to be at home but at least for the time being that is beyond one's power to achieve. It is not that what is desired is unattainable *per se*, but that we do not have the wherewithal to realise it.

On the other hand Generativity is full of zeal. Life is good and all sorts of achievements are possible. Here we find the student who has just been informed that she has won a scholarship to the college of her choice so that her future appears assured. She is plunged into a state of joyfulness. Here we can expect to find a contestant in the Olympic games who has just won a gold medal, and the mother who has just given birth and holds her baby for the first time.

Here too we find the research scientist who has just made a new and important discovery and is full of enthusiasm, ready to embark on the task of revealing it to the world.

Recently television news programmes showed the reactions of NASA scientists on receiving their first pictures from the space craft which had been sent to observe the planet Pluto. Their euphoria made it quite plain they were in Generativity as they celebrated this joint achievement.

When in Generativity the world is our oyster and we are confident of being able to fulfill all reasonable wishes. But in Self-Abasement however much change is desired we feel a lack of the wherewithal to bring it into effect.

Nevertheless hope is not ruled out. This is what distinguishes -4:Self-Abasement from the next step down namely -5: Despair.

CHAPTER 33

Despair and Emancipation

Next we come to +5:Emancipation and -5:Despair, describing spiritual states which are at the two extremes while still retaining a sense of ego, the personal centre of consciousness, the awareness of 'I/me'. These are experiences of being in heaven and hell.

Emancipation is characterised by a sense of liberation in which the very concept of problems just does not exist. Actions are spontaneous and there is contact with the source of inner intuitive wisdom producing a sense of wholeness as well as communion with the natural world in which the relationship is one of harmony.

By contrast Despair feels like a spiritual desert in which one has been abandoned by all sources of guidance and help, both inner and outer. It is a state of overwhelm in which one is utterly powerless, with nothing left to cling to for help and succour. Solutions and hope do not exist. Here we find the person who sees suicide as the only way out of the situation in which he finds himself. In Despair life is not worth living whereas in Emancipation life could not be more wonderful.

The unexpected death of one's spouse could plunge a person temporarily into a state of -5:Despair. Grief is at -4:Self-Abasement, but sudden unexpected bere-avement is worse, the shock taking a person even lower on the Scale than grief. This is the depth to which the spirit can sink while still retaining a sense of one's own identity. Here are utter depression, failure and alien-ation, an absence of hope and the wish to end one's life. At -4:Self-Abasement there remains the possibility that circumstances may change or help will arrive, but at -5: Despair all hope of relief has gone.

+5:Emancipation is the direct opposite. The spirit is exuberant, free, whole and inspirational. Here we might find the person who walks alone in the countryside and feels his spirit uplifted by its beauty and peacefulness. Here too is the scientist who suddenly realises the solution to a problem on which he has been working for years, sending him into a state of spiritual awe at the beauty and rightness of his discovery.

This is also one of the stages which can be experienced when meditating because of its sense of spiritual acceptance. It is at this level that Buddhist monks aim to conduct their everyday lives, although when engaged in formal meditation their aim is to reach the next stage which is +6:Transpersonalization.

On the down side this pair is associated with heroin addiction. To have a sure way of transporting oneself into a haven of peace and serenity merely by taking a drug, must be very attractive especially to those whose lives have been overshadowed by tragedy and despondence. The first dose takes people into spiritual bliss at +5:Emancipation which must seem like heaven, the answer to everything.

The trouble is that heroin's effect on the body's chemistry is highly addictive and very soon the drug becomes necessary, because without it the user is taken from heaven in +5:Emancipation across the Scale into hell in its opposite at -5:Despair. The result is a constant demand for the drug.

The problem is exacerbated by the fact that when in Despair people have no inner resources left with which to lift themselves out of the situation which is entirely controlled at a chemical level. It is no wonder they will do anything to obtain the next fix. Their life is lived entirely in this particular pair on the Scale, and overcoming the addiction requires an enormous effort of will.

While 4 are about the extremes of doing, what a person can and cannot change or achieve, 5 are about the extremes of being, the state of one's soul.

CHAPTER 34

Depersonalization and Transpersonalization

Finally we come to the ego-less pair -6:Depersonalization and +6:Transpersonalization. Both come into the category of altered states of consciousness, ASC's, and are difficult to describe to anyone who has not experienced an egoless state in which the sense of 'I/me' is absent. The sense of oneself as an individual person separate from the rest of creation, has completely disappeared.

In -6:Depersonalization the sense of self has shattered and disintegrated. While -5:Despair allows a person to cry out: 'Why am I in this state? What have I done?', in Depersonalization there is no sense of

'I'or 'me' to be blamed or succoured. There is just experience and confusion. Unreality prevails. There is complete psychological breakdown. There is no coherence, no cohesion, nothing is connected to anything else. There is just experience. These are states that get labelled 'madness'.

The contemplation of suicide has already been discussed under -5:Despair. Someone might ask why it is not considered to be in -6: Depersonalization instead, since it expresses a desire for the extreme solution and surely no frame of mind can be worse.

The difference is in the sense of self. In -5:Despair there exists an ego which is aware and can decide to end it all in death and then carry out the deed. However in -6:Depersonalization there is no ego, no self identity, no sense of who it is that is having the experience and therefore no will. Horror and terror exist and are experienced but without any sense of an agent or experiencer. So there can be no decisions made or actions taken to relieve that suffering. It just is. In -5:Despair death is one way out but even that solution does not exist in -6:Depersonalization.

The opposite is +6:Transpersonalization, which is also egoless but by a very different process. The ego has been transcended producing a state of union with everything that exists. The relationship with nature and the universe is that of a seamless whole. The self and the environment are no longer separate entities in a relationship as was the case in +5:Emancipation because they are now one and the same.

The goal of meditation is to reach this blissful state in which a person feels at one with the whole of creation. It can also occur suddenly as the result of a major flash of insight, the 'ah-ha' experience, *satori* in Zen.

There are two different kinds of meditation and therefore two types of peak experience[1] which they can produce. Concentrative meditation such as focussing on the breath or a mantra, comes from Indian yoga and aims at ever deeper states of bliss, *samadhi*. A galvanic skin response (GSR) meter shows the skin resistance steadily rise to reach a plateau level. In addition Buddhism has mindfulness or insight meditation, for example on a koan, which aims to eliminate restrictive programmes from the psyche[2] via flashes of insight, *satori*, at which juncture the skin resistance suddenly drops to a low level followed by smooth variation in what can only be described as gentle floating.

Low/high skin resistance correlates with involvement/withdrawal respectively, and not with stress/relaxation as has commonly been assumed.[3]

Ian Marshall's therapeutic system Sequential Analysis — of which the Scale of Responses is just one part — consists of set procedures to be used in conjunction with a suitable GSR meter. When properly applied the method encourages therapeutic insights of the kind that are associated with a brief peak experience. This is provided the therapist has the necessary skills, the most fundamental of which is the ability to keep the client's attention focussed on the questions and away from both the meter and the therapist's personality. It is unfortunate that only one of the one hundred of so procedures has been published[4].

Many people report having had a peak-experience, perhaps when walking alone in beautiful countryside, or listening to music, or contemplating the innocence of a child's smile, or in a eureka moment having suddenly realized a remarkable solution to a puzzling challenge that has been nagging for some time. In these experiences the experiencer is no longer an individual but has become united with the universe. All is one. Such moments do not last long and are to be treaured.

However the will remains. So there is no problem about regaining the ego, the sense of self-identity, by descending back into +5 if that is required. After all, even meditators have to eat and wash and carry out daily tasks, none of which can be accomplished while in an egoless state since all of these activities require distinction between the doer and that which is done.

While in -6 the ego has disintegrated and there is no spiritual will left, in +6 the will remains intact. Although the ego has been transcended it can be resumed at will.

By way of illustration here is one of my own peak experiences. I was seventeen and it was just after the war when the beaches were opened up again for the first time for years. My mother and I were taking an easter break at Littlehampton. The tide was high, a gale was blowing, and the beach sloped down into the sea. Huge waves broke close to the shore. I was determined to go in. It was dangerous — a mistake and I could have been killed.

I watched as each wave approached and then dived beneath as its huge mass arched and broke above me. Then facing the shore it was necessary to lean back at an angle to counter the undertow. This was all so exhilarating it was as if the sea and I were playing a game of skills together, testing each other's strength.

Then came a flash of insight: When in the presence of a great force do not try to oppose it, but go along with it and make use of it.

From that moment it was as if the sea and I were no longer separate entities but were one in The Game. The Game was all that there was. Somehow the incoming waves continued to be monitored and split-second decisions made, but I was not conscious that it was I making those decisions. There was a sense of the rightness of the situation.

There were just serenity, harmony, and wholeness.

Eventually my body had had enough and the sense of self returned. I made my way carefully to the water's edge — no easy matter against the forward rush of waves towards the shoreline and the backward tug of undertow. Back on land I felt refreshed and invigorated.

The serenity of +6 is in stark contrast to the horror of -6. There are those that maintain that Depersonalization is a return to the trauma of being born[5], since the baby is presumably engulfed in physical stress and also possibly pain but has no sense of self identity and no concept of will. This leads to the conjecture that an infant's gradual development of a sense of self[6] is somehow related to the ascent from -6 up to -1.

Until a few decades ago psychology did not distinguish between these two egoless states with the result that both were treated as equally pathological. Transpersonalization was regarded as a return to the womb. Happily the spread of eastern practices in the west has given us a better understanding so that transcendence can now be perceived as the ego voluntarily relinquishing control to the inner transpersonal self[7].

The previous chapter included some comments on the use of heroin. While that drug is related to ±5, LSD typically sends the user into ±6. This is not an addictive drug like heroin and users tend to experience the egolessness of +6:Transpersonalization during the early part of the trip provided they are willing to let go, and if not then at least they get as far as +5:Emancipation. However if the drug is used in unsuitable circumstances then -6:Depersonalization can be the result. It was cases of this happening that prompted its relegation to the status of an illegal substance.

So what circumstances are unsuitable? First and foremost if an intended user does not have a strong and stable ego then that is too weak a springboard from which to transcend the ego and can lead to a cross-over to the minus side. Under this drug all experiences and emotions are exaggerated so the minus side is not where one would wish to be.

Next in importance LSD should not be ingested when there is any-thing playing upon the person's mind, because that also could trigger a flip across to the minus side. The environment must be free from interruptions and the company trustworthy, because this drug weakens the natural safety barrier which normally prevents us from contacting material buried in the unconscious mind. This last fact was what attracted scientific researchers to explore its uses as a psychotherapeutic tool in the 1950's and early 1960's before it became illegal.[8]

Finally there should be someone present who is stable and capable of helping participants who get into trouble. This might involve, for example, reassuring them that what they have taken is a hallucinogen and that its effect will wear off.

I cannot comment on any of the more recent social drugs because their psychological effects have not been observed under scientifically reliable conditions.

CHART 4

The Scale of Responses
expanded version

Negative		Positive
NEUTRALITY 0 (Vagrant, Uninvolved)		
Weariness (Boredom, Reluctance) Disregard (Ignore) **SELF-ASSERTION** (Competitor; Ambition to impress or excel) Insistence (Domineering, Demanding, Prejudiced) Impatience (Disgust)	1	Alertness (General interest) Attentiveness (Focused perception) **EXPLORATION** (Spectator, Researcher; Curiosity) Fairness (Receptiveness) Tolerance
Blame (Disparage, Protest) Threat (Anger) **ATTACK** (Sadist, Enemy, Psychopath; Cruelty) Envy (Spite, Begrudge) Resentment (Grievance)	2	Praise Support (Agreement, Assent) **CO-OPERATION** (Citizen, Colleague; Amiability) Admiration Gratitude
Suspiciousness Evasiveness (Shyness, Secrecy) **RETREAT** (Fugitive; Fatigue, Fear) Callousness (Autism, Frigidity) Theatricality (Hysteria, Coquetry)	3	Trust Frankness **PARTICIPATION** (Friend; Gregariousness) (Lover; Sex) Empathy (Understanding, Attraction) Intimacy (Informality, Caresses)
Shame (Inadequacy, Degradation, Guilt) Ingratiation (Obsequious, Deceitful, Brainwashed, Prostitution) **SELF-ABASEMENT** (Masochist; Self-contempt) Grief (Mourning, Loss, Emptiness) Nostalgia (Pining for the absent)	4	Enthusiasm (Zeal, Ardour, Intercourse) Commitment (Generosity, Orgasm, Conception) **GENERATIVITY** (Craftsman, Helper, Parent; Devotion) Joy (Celebration, Birth, Abundance) Gracefulness (Style and taste in the present)
Regression (Return to infantility, Decay, Starvation) Discouragement (Depression, Futility, Retardation) **DESPAIR** (Failure, Suicide; Abdication) Universal rejection (Alienation, Abhorrence) Delusion	5	Growth (Integration, Digestion) Exuberance (Spontaneity, Zest, Energy) **EMANCIPATION** (Freeman; Evolution) (Humanist; Love of nature) Universal acceptance (Wholeness) Inspiration (Intuition, Genius)
Grandiosity (Inflation) Confusion (Unreality, Delirium, Splitting, Ego damage) **DEPERSONALIZATION** (Schizophrenic; Ego loss) Invasion (Possessed, Catatonic, Cosmic horror and dread) Spiritual extinction (Apathy, Vegetable)	6	Humility (Spiritual powerlessness of the ego, Integrity) Ecstasy (Positive spiritual experience) **TRANSPERSONALIZATION** (Mystic; Ego transcendence) Union (Fusion, Cosmic love and reverence) Spiritual fulfilment (Tao, Harmony, Serenity, Wisdom)

CHAPTER 35

More Detail

The Scale of Reponses as depicted in the Charts 1, 2 and 3 was designed by Marshall in 1969, shortly to be followed by the expanded version in Chart 4. In fact there were several slightly different versions of the expanded chart and that which is reproduced here is the one I prefer.

The expanded version has its advantages and disadvantages. On the helpful side it gives some idea of the range of responses that constitute each of the thirteen different categories or 'steps'. Above and below the capitalised items are responses which can be regarded as tending towards the next box, up or down. For example in the SELF-ABASE-MENT section Shame and Ingratiation are placed above the main item to indicate that they are not far from RETREAT, while Grief and Nostalgia are closer to DESPAIR.

The principle of pairing opposites across the page has been pre-served. The brackets after each capitalised item contain (a) the role of the person who experiences that response and (b) the manifestation of that response. For example EXPLORATION (Spectator, Researcher; Curiosity). A person in an exploratory mood may be in the role of a spectator or a researcher, and the mood manifests in the activity of being curious.

The disadvantage of the expanded version is its complexity which can be misleading — a good reason for not including it in the previous chapters. The Step-By-Step principle which will be described in the chapter 'One Step at a Time', goes from one manifestation in a category to one manifestation in the next category; it does NOT go step-by-step through all five items in each category. For example one may go from Shyness (-3) to Shame (-4) or from Admiration (+2) to Trust (+3).

Similarly the One Up mechanism and the Knight's Move which are described in succeeding chapters, do not discriminate between the various items described as belonging to any one level.

For this reason I have found that the simpler version of the Scale with just its thirteen steps is more useful as a practical tool in spite of the extra theoretical information contained in the expanded version. It is suggested that the reader continue to use Chart 2, and refer to Chart 4 only when in need of more detailed information concerning what a particular level might include.

To illustrate the point this chapter concludes with some examples in which responses are analysed in terms of the thirteen items of Chart 2.

Each of the thirteen responses on the Scale is appropriate in certain circumstances. A person at maximum psychological health would be one who is flexible, capable of entering whichever response is appropriate at the time, whether that be on the plus or the minus side, and also, importantly, capable of leaving it again.

It might be thought that there could never be an appropriate situation for experiencing the extreme of -6:Depersonalization, but this would be incorrect. Consider an accident victim who is rendered unconscious. As he begins to gain consciousness there is a sense of unreality and confusion without any grasp of the sense of his own identity. This may be a brief experience but it is appropriate in the circumstances.

In describing these six pairs of opposite responses we have passed through what can be considered three bands. First there were the personal ego-centred responses of ±1, then the interpersonal or social ones, ending with those which involve the spirit at ±5 and ±6.

The chapters which follow will describe ways in which these various responses are inter-related forming a continuum, and will also show that this system is complete. This chapter ends with some examples illustrating how to identify responses on the Scale.

Example 1

A would-be robber brandishing a gun, enters a bank and demands money. Prima, the clerk, hands over the cash in her till.

Is the robber in -1:Self-Assertion or -2:Attack? He enters the bank brandishing a gun as a threat. This puts him in -2:Attack. But Prima's apparent co-operation enables him to relax a little. There is no need to threaten any more as long as he maintains control of the situation. So he may now have moved into -1:Self-Assertion.

What about Prima? Is she really in +2:Co-operation? Although clearly she co-operates by handing over the money, that is not where her true response lies but is only where she is pretending to be in order to keep the robber happy and save her own life. She is certainly not experiencing any 'degree of acceptance' of the situation (see the note under Chart 3), which eliminates any response on the plus side. So +2:Co-operation is not her true response. She is somewhere on the minus side of the chart.

Is Prima afraid, or is she thinking 'I cannot deal with this; I shall get blamed for the bank's loss'? Or maybe she is looking for an opportunity to thwart the thief. If afraid then she is in -3:Retreat because psychologically she is backing away. If she feels that somehow she is letting the bank down and will be blamed then this indicates -4:Self-Abasement. Finally if determined to turn the tables on him then her state of mind is in -1:Self-Assertion.

Whichever, Prima hands over the cash. This illustrates the fact that it is not always easy to determine a person's true response simply by observing behaviour.

DIAGRAM 2
Bank Robber

Robber	**His Perception of Prima**
-2: Attack (enters with gun)	
. . . . +2: Co-operation (hands over cash)	
-1: Self-Assertion (in control)	

Prima's True Response

-3: Retreat (afraid)

or   -4: Self-Abasement (self-blame)

or   -1: Self-Assertion (determined)

Example 2

A certain tennis player engages in a friendly game. This locates him at +2:Co-operation. However if he feels that his opponent has a chance of winning then his mood may change. He studies the opponent's tactics (+1:Exploration) and counters them (-1:Self-Assertion). On the other hand if playing in a tournament and winning is important then he will be determined to defeat the other player (-2:Attack).

DIAGRAM 3
Tennis Player

+2: Co-operation (friendly game)

-1: Self-Assertion (employs tactics) . . . . . . +1: Exploration (observes opponent)

-2: Attack (to defeat opponent)

Example 3

Immediately following the death of his wife Heather, Eric is distraught. Their neighbour Fearne, a family friend, is sorrowful.

Eric's reaction is deeper than Fearne's. He has lost his life partner and is temporarily devastated. This puts him in -5:Despair for the time being as he is completely unable to function. -4:Self-Abasement is the usual level for grief as bereavement is a situation which cannot be changed no matter how much we would wish it, so we would expect him to enter this level soon. Fearne was not so close to Heather so her response is not as deep as grief, but she is still affected. This puts her in -3:Retreat since her inner self is temporarily restricted from involvement with the everyday world by her sorrow.

DIAGRAM 4
Grief

Eric	Fearne
-5: Despair (distraught)	-3: Retreat (sorrowful)
-4: Self-Abasement (grief)	

Example 4

A teenager awaits the results of her exams in a state of anxiety. She needs good grades in order to be able to attend the university of her choice in preparation for her desired career as a lawyer. When the results are announced her grades are all A's. She is over the moon with delight. Her future is assured.

DIAGRAM 5
Exam Results

-3: Retreat (anxiety, fear)

major jump to: +4: Generativity (joyful, celebratory)

CHAPTER 36

Personal Norm

If asked to describe someone whom we know well the answer usually contains more than just a simple description of that person's physical appearance. Also included would probably be that person's occupation, interests and personality. Here we are concerned with the last of these, personality, for that includes attitude and reactions.

Think of a friend, relative or colleague and immediately certain characteristics come to mind. One person is quiet, shy, retiring, always polite, ready to help someone in need. Another is friendly, a good sport, takes risks, is outspoken and sometimes unintentionally rubs people up the wrong way. A third is secretive, sly and cannot be trusted.

Each has his or her customary way of reacting to others and of responding to situations, and it would surprise us if, on some occasion, any were to react in a radically different manner. We expect them to stick to their own personal norm. We do not expect a quiet person suddenly to flare up in a temper or a self-assured individual to remain silent in the face of another's insult or criticism, although these reactions do occasionally happen.

Most people seem to have what can be described as their normal position on the Scale of Responses, their most frequent response to whatever is going on around them. We have probably all met the shy, self-effacing individual at -3:Retreat, the bossy one at -1:Self-Assertion, the one who is easy to get along with at +2:Co-operation, and the aggressive type at -2:Attack. In fact any discussion of personality and temperament must be influenced by the position on the chart of that individual's norm.

In general people do not stay at their norm on the Scale all of the time though this is not unknown. Life throws all sorts of things at us and we respond accordingly. Circumstances occur which evoke other reactions, and possibly a variety of different reactions in succession. But it has been observed that *in general a change in response is fea-*

*tured on the Scale as a move from one position to the next, in other
words one up, one down, or across to the opposite.*

So someone whose norm is at +2:Co-operation might also be
expected frequently to show interest (+1:Exploration) and empathy
(+3:Participation) and to respond to negativity with protest (-2:Attack).
The other responses on the chart are available to this person, given
suitable stimuli, but the personal norm and those responses which are
immediately adjacent will occur most frequently.

Example 1

Ernestine is a social worker. She chose this occupation because she
sees it as an opportunity to do some good in the world. In her spare time
she is involved with charity work and supports the green movement.
Her friends and relatives find her always willing to help them out when
in trouble, but they fear she will wear herself out eventually with the
way in which she throws herself so readily into everything undertaken.

Ernestine's customary attitude of devoting herself wholeheartedly
to whatever she undertakes, places her norm at +3:Participation.

On a day when she feels a bit under the weather her heart may
not be entirely in her job, so she just jogs along in +2:Co-operation
endeavouring to carry out her tasks adequately. This is one step away
from her norm. On a really good day when everything seems to go
right, Ernestine feels capable of anything and her enthusiasm places
her in +4:Generativity, also one step from her norm. But if something
goes badly wrong her immediate reaction is disbelief. Now disbelief
is a form of disconnection, which locates her in -3:Retreat, her norm's
opposite. Eventually she recovers her usual position in +3:Participation
having dealt with the unfortunate situation.

DIAGRAM 6
Ernestine's Norm

```
                              +2: Co-operation (jogs along)
-3: Retreat (disbelief) . . . . . . . . . . . . . . . . . . +3: Participation (Ernestine's norm)
                              +4: Generativity (enthusiasm)
```

Unfortunately the people that Ernestine helps are not always happy with her efforts because what she does is not necessarily what they want. The trouble is that she seldom goes into +1:Exploration in order to assess what would truly benefit them. She always 'knows best'.

This reminds me of the tale I heard recently of a blind man whose wife left him outside a shop while she went inside. He stood patiently on the pavement facing the road but when she came out of the shop he was on the opposite pavement on the other side of the road. A 'helpful' passerby had grabbed hold and steered him across without bothering to find out if that was where he wanted to be. This is a case of not being in +1:Exploration!

Example 2

Grace is a shy little girl, the only child of a single mother. The school bullies pick on her and make her life a misery leaving her to feel worthless because she cannot cope. She tells mother who is not up to facing the perpetrators or their parents and instead tries to comfort Grace and give her courage. This has the effect of bringing out the child's anger against her bullies. But of course as soon as she is back at school she feels bad again.

Mother recognises the child's loneliness and buys her a little dog called Gruff for company which turns out to be her saviour. Pet dogs are non-judgmental, and Grace is well aware that she is mistress in Gruff's eyes and that he harbours not a speck of criticism against her. The two of them adore each other and play together happily for hours.

Were it not for Gruff it is quite possible that Grace would eventually have deteriorated psychologically into self-harm and even suicide. Sadly this does indeed sometimes happen to those who are bullied.

Grace's shyness and reticence reveal that her norm is -3:Retreat. When bullied she feels worthless and unable to cope, which is a step down into -4:Self-Abasement. However when talking with mother this releases her anger at the bullies as she goes up into -2:Attack. This is at least a step in the right direction. Nevertheless the norm returns.

Her relationship with Gruff changes everything. Here is a playmate with whom she can share her very being as she crosses over from her norm into its opposite +3:Participation. This new pattern means that the downward trend on the minus side of the Scale has lost its potency since any lack of self-worth produced by the bullies is offset by her new playmate. She has been saved from further descent into -5:Despair.

DIAGRAM 7
Grace's Norm

-2: Attack (anger)
-3: Retreat (Grace's norm) . . . . +3: Participation (plays with Gruff)
-4: Self-Abasement (feels worthless)
-5: Despair (*situation avoided*)

Example 3

It is possible to have two personal norms. For example a person with bipolar disorder spends several weeks with a norm high up on the ladder, followed by weeks in its direct opposite. There is a see-sawing between the two. The norm pair may be +4:Generativity and -4: Self-Abasement, but further research is needed to establish the pattern and to find out whether the responses immediately above and below are also available.

This chapter may have given the impression that personal norms are fixed for life until a trauma occurs, but this is not the case. It can be changed up or down by life's experiences, especially major ones such as injury, a sudden change in circumstances, a near-death experience, regular meditation practice, psychological therapy, or a sudden enlightening insight into one's own attitudes and behaviour.

Then there are people with more than one norm, depending on the environment in which they find themselves. For example the person who is the life and soul of the party when with friends but domineering in the home and subservient towards authority. If these are permanent patterns then we could regard them as separate norms rather than as movements on the Scale. They would then indicate subpersonalities.[1]

We all have subpersonalities. This is a complex topic and will be considered in a later chapter.

CHAPTER 37

One Step At A Time

Before going any further the sense in which the terms 'up' and 'down' will be used needs clarification. We started off with thirteen responses in the form of a ladder (Chart 1) the top of which is at +6. This was then folded in half for Chart 2 but the top is still +6. So 'up' goes from -6 through 0 to +6, which means that on the plus side of Chart 2 'up' is from 0 to +6 and 'down' is from +6 to 0. On the right-hand side of Chart 2 'up' means down and 'down' means up (Diagram 8).

DIAGRAM 8

UP

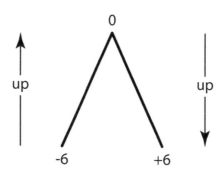

The meaning of 'up' in the two halves of the Scale.

In the previous chapter it was seen that a departure from the norm is usually one step up, down or across. However circumstances can occur which cause us to range more widely, but there is still a tendency to move one step at a time. In fact this one-step-at-a-time phenomenon can be observed in most fluid situations regardless of whether or not the personal norm is involved.

Example 1

At a public lecture a member of the audience tries to pay attention but becomes bored.

Paying attention is in +1:Exploration. Boredom is a recognition that all is not as we would wish and therefore belongs on the minus side of the Scale. There is no suggestion of attack or deliberate withdrawal so it is in -1:Self-Assertion. This member of the audience has flipped across from +1 to its opposite in -1.

Example 2

Consider the case of a traveller consulting a train time-table. Provided there is no other factor affecting his mood, our seeker of information is probably at +1:Exploration regardless of where his personal norm would be. Say someone else comes along offering constructive help, then our subject, who starts in +1:Exploration, could go up into a state of +2:Co-operation. Or perhaps he found the required information, filed it for future use and, having nothing else to do for the time being, goes down into 0:Neutrality.

The third possibility namely from +1:Exploration into its opposite, -1:Self-Assertion, might be evoked if the time-table proves to be difficult to follow and he decides to take a more active line and telephones the information clerk at the station. When the clerk turns out to be unhelpful he fumes. He has gone one step further from -1:Self-Assertion into -2:Attack even if remaining outwardly controlled.

It is not always easy to assess a person's position on the chart because that which is being experienced inwardly may not be overtly expressed. Indeed it is possible to put on a deliberate act to conceal one's inner feelings. How often is a seething inner resentment concealed behind an outer appearance of calmness and friendship? It is the person's inner state which determines the true position on the Scale, not the assumptions that others project on to that individual.

Another confusing factor is the superficial similarity which some responses have to each other. For example, does silence indicate 0:Neutrality or -3:Retreat? The answer can usually be found by con-

DIAGRAM 9

The Train Time-Table

0: Neutrality
(nothing happening)

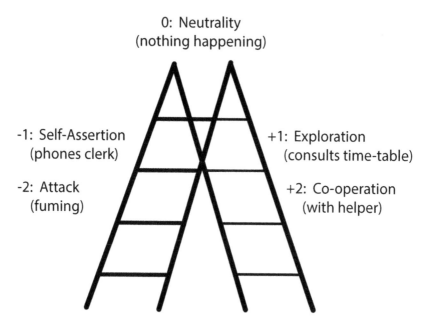

-1: Self-Assertion
(phones clerk)

+1: Exploration
(consults time-table)

-2: Attack
(fuming)

+2: Co-operation
(with helper)

sidering what other response is close. So, if a moment ago that person was angry (-2:Attack) then the chances are that the silence indicates withdrawal or being non-plussed, which belong in -3:Retreat. On the other hand if the previous situation had been one of +1:Exploration or -1:Self-Assertion then the silence is probably just a temporary hesitation and indicates 0:Neutrality.

It was stated above that changes usually happen one step at a time. Exceptions to this general rule occur when something momentous suddenly happens, and then a person may jump to quite a different place on the chart. A sudden severe trauma can plunge someone down into -5:Despair ('this is the end of my world') or even further into -6: Depersonalization (confusion, unreality). At the other extreme a sudden major insight can produce a peak experience, an instantaneous transcendence of the sense of self (+6:Transpersonalization), the result of what is known as *satori* in Zen. 'Satori is the sudden flashing into consciousness of a new truth, hitherto undreamed of' (D.T.Suzuki). [1]

This altered state of consciousness tends to be brief, followed by a fairly rapid one-step-at-a-time return to normal. By contrast after a trauma the climb back up-scale may be a long and laborious journey, and the individual may never succeed in returning to the previous norm. Going up-scale is generally a slower process than going down. This will be illustrated in the next two examples which describe a grieving process and recovery from a serious accident.

Similarly stepping across from a negative to its positive opposite is not as common as the other way round. We are probably all familiar with the situation in which trust (+3:Participation) is betrayed causing a sudden flip across into suspiciousness and secrecy (-3:Retreat), but I suspect that a sudden flip from suspiciousness straight into trust without going slowly all the way round through 0 to get there, is almost unknown.

The exception is from -1:Self-Assertion across to its opposite +1:Exploration. If someone tries to get his own way and fails, he might just try to find out why. After all +1 and -1 are close to each other on the Scale, separated only by Neutrality.

The next two examples illustrate the slow one-step-at-a-time climb back up-scale following a trauma. First to be described is the grieving process associated with bereavement, and that is followed by a case of recovery from serious injury in an accident.

Example 3

First a lengthy grieving process will be described and then it will be analysed in terms of steps on the Scale.

Patience is in her early 70's and her husband has just died after a short and unexpected illness. They had no children and there is no close family member able to take his place in her life. He was her sole companion and support.

Patience suffers from arthritis so she relied on him to drive her to the shops. However during his short illness she discovered that the local grocery shop would deliver — one problem solved — but there are other essential household goods that one needs to buy from time to time. Right now her life needs re-organising but she is in no mental state to take that on board.

Initially she is stunned, devastated. Her whole world seems to have collapsed around her. She feels alone and helpless. Fortunately neighbour Benedict comes to the rescue. He is an active man in his 40's, good at getting things done. Although he recognises he is not much good at coping with other people's emotions he can still offer help in a practical form. So he takes on the funeral arrangements, assists her with the task of informing friends and relatives, and offers to drive her to the shops on Saturdays.

This helps her over the first shock, at which point the reality of her loss hits home and grief takes over. She cries a great deal, especially when on her own, but endeavours to stifle her tears in front of neighbours.

One such neighbour is Felicity, a well-meaning individual who feels that it is her duty to cheer Patience up. So she visits regularly with cheerful chat and advice about getting on with one's life. Patience politely manages to smile, but the two of them are not on the same wavelength which makes Patience feel even more isolated. What she really wants is to cry while someone puts a comforting arm around her shoulders so that she can feel her grief is understood and shared.[2]

She dwells on her memories and soon begins to have disturbing thoughts. Could she have done something that would have saved his life? Did she make it clear to him that she loved him? And then there are all those feelings of regret for past quarrels and for failures to put things right while there was still a chance. Once again Felicity is no help. All she does is tell Patience that these thoughts are nonsense which, of course, does not make them go away.

As time passes Patience becomes more accustomed to coping with the everyday chores of life on her own with occasional help from Benedict, but she is nowhere near ready to resume a normal social life. Having realised that Felicity makes her feel worse she pretends to be out whenever that well-meaning neighbour calls round. In fact she has withdrawn into herself. The household chores, the shopping and the bills, are all she can cope with right now. Life is flat, it is just ticking over.

Slowly a little energy begins to return. She starts to take in events and circumstances in the world around her, and in so doing becomes aware of the contrast between the apparently fulfilled lives of others and her own state of loss. Why did this have to happen? What did she do to deserve it? The happiness of others even makes her feel envious, and she feels critical of Felicity for not understanding her needs. She has always believed that one should endeavour not to become a burden on others so she keeps these thoughts to herself and they fester within.

Gradually common-sense prevails and she comes to accept that, although the death of her husband cannot be reversed, nevertheless life has to go on and there is no good reason for not making the best of the situation in which she finds herself. At first Patience has to force herself to attend a local social club, but very soon the companionship she encounters gets through to her and she begins actually to enjoy it. At last she is on the road to becoming herself once again.

Felicity observes the improvement and congratulates herself for having helped Patience pull through, though at the same time being somewhat puzzled by the period when the widow appeared always to be out. Benedict has become a good friend and continues to be of occasional practical help, but Patience can now stand on her own feet, developing new interests and hobbies, making new contacts, living her own independent life.

What can be said about this process in relation to the Scale of Responses? First of all it has taken many months, possible a couple of years, so the account given above is a mere sketch. In reality the transition from one stage to the next is not so clear-cut as the brief account above would appear to imply.

What is happening here is a slow progression through a succession of temporary personal norms, each one a step up on the previous one. As with any personal norm there are brief excursions into the states above and below with a return to whatever was the temporary personal norm at that time. This makes any boundaries between the stages of the recovery process fuzzy. Transition from one personal norm to the one above is gradual, with an ever-increasing preponderance of excursions into the upper response and a slow decrease in occurrences of the one below, until eventually a new temporary norm is reached. And so it goes on to the next stage. The sketch which has been given here omits all these fuzzy details and just describes the general trend.

First of all there is a period of spiritual shock, of devastation and profound loss. Her world has collapsed around her with everything that was familiar gone or altered. Her state of mind is -5:Despair. She cannot cope with everyday life and desperately needs someone to take charge.

This gives way fairly quickly to grief as the reality of her situation strikes home. Grief is a state of mind in which one is powerless to reverse what has happened, and is found in -4:Self-Abasement. She is frequently reduced to tears and desperately needs someone with whom she can share her grief. She questions her own role during her husband's brief illness and blames herself for all sorts of imagined failures in his care and in their relationship.

Next Patience withdraws into herself for a quiet life, managing to cope with daily life on her own and with Benedict's occasional help, but unable to cope outside the daily routine. She is now in -3:Retreat. She even avoids Felicity's attempts to intrude by pretending to be out. Her life is just ticking over.

Being on her own so much she can mull things over, and this is when she becomes aware of the contrast between her current life and those of other people. They enjoy themselves while she is stuck here at home trying to come to terms with her loss. Envy sets in. And her neighbour Felicity has been no help. Her inner state of mind is now -2:Attack even though, as a naturally well-behaved lady, she would not actually give vent to her feelings of resentment publicly.

As time goes on Patience comes to recognise that these resentments achieve nothing and that bereavement cannot be reversed. She needs to live her own life and begins to take control. At first she has to force herself to attend the local social club which places her at -1:Self-Assertion, and then she crosses over to the opposite at +1:Exploration as she begins to get into the swing of activities and makes new friends. This leads on to positive enjoyment, +2:Co-operation, and she is well on her way to establishing a new permanent norm for herself. (Diagram 10 overleaf)

In the grieving process it is to be expected that a person's temporary norm slowly rises one step at a time until reaching that individual's natural personal norm. This is not necessarily the same as before the bereavement occurred but it is likely to be close. The one-step-at-a-time process is natural and cannot be hurried, because it is necessary fully to express and work through one's state of mind at each stage. When this is done a person is automatically ready to go up to the next rung of the ladder, a stage which in turn must also be fully expressed and worked through, and so on. The trouble with Felicity's approach was that she wanted to hurry the process along. Well, that simply does not work. Benedict, on the other hand, did exactly what was required. He unburdened Patience of certain practical matters so that her psyche could take its natural course through her range of emotions.

This whole process would have taken many months with the account given here being just a brief outline. The story describes a progression of temporary norms slowly rising up-scale. Provided there are no further traumas the general trend up-scale over an extended period of time is to be expected.

DIAGRAM 10
Patience's Grieving Process

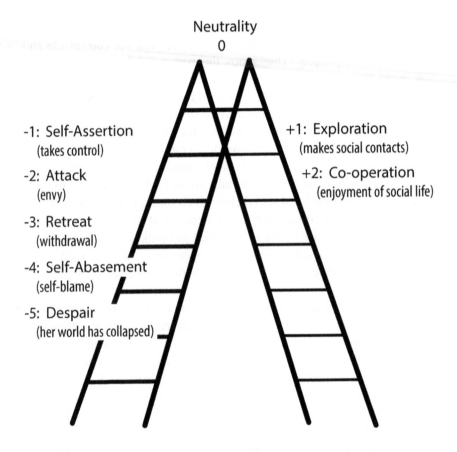

Neutrality
0

-1: Self-Assertion
(takes control)

+1: Exploration
(makes social contacts)

-2: Attack
(envy)

+2: Co-operation
(enjoyment of social life)

-3: Retreat
(withdrawal)

-4: Self-Abasement
(self-blame)

-5: Despair
(her world has collapsed)

Bereavement counsellors who are trained to facilitate this lengthy process are aware of a particularly tricky stage. This is at -2:Attack. In Patience's case it took the form of envy of those who had not suffered bereavement as well as a critical attitude towards Felicity. With some clients this stage can be much more challenging. Perhaps they rail about their doctor, blaming him for the death of the loved one and threatening to sue for malpractice. For counsellors and friends alike the temptation is to try to allay the anger and calm the person down. This might help the helpers who find anger difficult to cope with, but it does not help the bereaved person deal with those feelings.

Counsellors are trained to cope with strong anger, but friends and neighbours not so. An attempt to stifle the grieving person's feelings will not make them go away. It will only prolong the overall process and will probably produce a temporary regression into -3:Retreat as the bereaved person shrinks into silence. -2:Attack has to be worked through to its natural completion just like every other stage in order to progress to the next step up. The exception is if Attack happens to be that person's natural norm, in which case the process is likely to stop there.

Example 4

24-year-old Nelson leads a very full and enjoyable life. One day he is riding his pride and joy, a motorbike, when he comes into collision with a car rendering him unconscious. He is rushed to hospital where he has an operation. As the anaesthetic wears off and dim awareness returns a medic informs him that he is in hospital, he has had an accident and he will be all right. Everything feels like a dream but these words are reassuring so he is able just to lie there and let things happen.

Very soon he discovers he has lost a leg. This is devastating. It will completely change his life. No more motorbike for sure. He can still do his office job and make a living, but no more football or walking holidays, and he fears no more girls and sex. In a wheelchair he will be unable to cope with living alone in his bachelor flat and will have to rely on his parents once again. A desolate life lies ahead. Why could he not just have died?

Then comes the self-blame. If only he had not driven so fast. If only he had paid more attention to the other traffic on the road instead of thinking about his girl-friend. What if she is no longer interested now that he is crippled? Lying there alone he would rather his friends, and especially his girl-friend, do not visit as he fears their reactions on seeing him in this damaged state.

These thoughts lead to anger with the car driver whom he concludes could not have been looking where he was going. Nelson is also angry with himself for being so stupid as to bring all this upon himself.

A prosthetic limb is now ready and he has to learn how to use it. This takes courage and dedication but eventually the skill is mastered and he leaves hospital in a wheelchair, wearing his new limb.

Back in his parents' home he has to learn how to get around. He also has to learn new ways of relating to people, partly because they are unsure how to deal with this physically different young man. His friends are still there for him but he can no longer participate in their games of football. Also his girl-friend has cooled off though she is still around as a friend. However he enjoys what activities he can.

Nelson's former happy life-style puts his norm at +3:Participation. Then came the accident, following which he passed through a similar one-step-at-a-time process to that which Patience experienced. Once again in reality the steps are not as clear-cut as they might seem from the brief description above which is a condensed picture of the general trend in his mood over several months, the progression up-scale of his temporary norms over time. Once again at each stage there are actually many fluctuations from the temporary norm, producing a much more fluid and vacillating process than this account might suggest.

His process starts from one step lower than Patience, at -6: Depersonalization while recovering consciousness in hospital after the operation, when he has not yet recovered a grasp on his own identity and everything seems unreal like a dream. On getting back in touch with who he is, the discovery of the loss of his leg produces a sense of devastation along with the realization of all the activities that will no longer be available to him. Unable to face what lies ahead (-5:Despair), why could he not have died?

If only he had not been driving so fast. If only he had paid more attention to the traffic instead of day-dreaming about his girl-friend. All this self-blame locates him in -4:Self-Abasement. The picture of himself as a cripple makes him unwilling to let his friends visit him in hospital. This is -3:Retreat.

Being on his own a lot he has time to ponder the event that brought about his tragedy, and this leads to anger – anger at the other driver whom he assumes was not looking where he was going, and anger at himself for his own careless stupidity. He is now at -2:Attack.

With the arrival of the prosthetic limb he has to make an effort to learn how to use it. Determination to achieve this locates him in -1:Self-Assertion. Eventually having mastered the skill he is ready to leave hospital.

There may be a period of 0:Neutrality or he may skip straight across to the opposite in +1:Exploration. Either way the next recognisable stage is learning how to adapt to his parents' home while getting about in a wheelchair, and learning new ways of relating to people who see him now as a different person. Eventually he gets used to these changed circumstances while the company of parents and friends lifts him into +2:Co-operation. But his girl-friend's cooling off and the loss of activities like football and sex which meant so much to him, mean that his old norm of +3:Participation is probably now out of reach. His permanent personal norm is now at +2:Co-operation.

DIAGRAM 11
Nelson's Motorbike Accident

+3:Participation (Nelson's former norm)
accident
-6:Depersonalization (unreality)
-5:Despair (loss of leg)
-4:Self-Abasement (self-blame)
-3:Retreat (unwilling to be seen)
-2:Attack (anger)
-1:Self-Assertion (learning to use limb)
+1:Exploration (adapting)
+2:Co-operation (company)

One very important feature of this whole scenario lies in Nelson's experiences during the initial emergence from the anaesthetic when in a state of unreality and utter dependence (-6:Depersonalization). Psychologically this is akin to starting life all over again. The victim is utterly dependent with no control whatever, and has regressed to having the vulnerabilities of a newborn infant. Anyone who helps him now is in danger of having 'parent' projected onto them.

This is normal and in itself not a problem. It only becomes so if, at a later stage in the recovery process, this parent figure fails to live up to the 'good enough parent' role. This is because the patient's rise up-scale step-by-step is accompanied by psychological development mirroring that of a child growing up towards adulthood, including dependency on the 'parent'. The same emotional traumas can be absorbed by the patient that would normally affect a growing child – all happening within the unconscious recesses of the mind and therefore not open to self-control.[3]

In Nelson's case this was not a problem because the medic who took on a parental role by reassuring him after the operation, represented the National Health system which continued to give excellent care throughout his recovery.

Compare this with Patience for whom Benedict put himself into the father role – albeit unintentionally – when she desperately needed a parent figure to guide her. He maintained this role and did not let her down. Contrast Felicity's behaviour which was quite inappropriate for someone in a childlike state of mind. Fortunately Felicity never had 'parent' projected onto her, for had this been the case Patience would have been very upset by her failure to provide genuine support.

If people allow themselves to become parent substitutes by taking control, or seeming to do so, or by offering advice and help, then it is vital that they honour the role and remain dependable at least until the patient has recovered some psychological independence. However at the same time helpers need to be careful not to become 'parental' by talking down to their patients. Although at the early stages of recovery patients have the same emotional vulnerability as developing infants, nevertheless they are still adults intellectually and will recognise and resent being patronised. This makes for a difficult path for helpers to tread, who are dealing with a patient that is intellectually adult but emotionally an infant (temporarily).

Example 5

Felix is a person who enjoys company and is easy to get on with. For some time he has been practising Transcendental Meditation[4]. First he gets into the rhythm of the practice by concentrating on his breath or on a mantra. The distractions of everyday life fall away and his mind calms. After a while he experiences a sense of expansion, and occasionally he goes into an ego-less state of serenity and unity with the whole of creation.

His permanent norm appears to be at +2:Co-operation, though if we knew more about him we might find it is at +3:Participation. Either way, getting into the rhythm is in +3:Participation because his whole being is absorbed in the activity. As his mind calms and is freed from distractions he is in +4:Generativity, the falling away of life's difficulties and problems. His sense of expansion is a spiritual experience and therefore an example of +5:Emancipation, and occasionally he reaches +6:Transpersonalization as he enters the ego-less state of oneness with the whole of creation.

When his meditation is over he returns step by step to his norm. With regular practice over time it would be expected that a person's norm will change to a position which is higher than before.

DIAGRAM 12
Felix's Meditation

+2: Co-operation (friendly, Felix's norm)
+3: Participation (into the rhythm)
+4: Generativity (no problems, no distractions)
+5: Emancipation (expansion)
+6: Transpersonalization (union)

This last example illustrates movement up-scale one step at a time, though different from the experiences of Patience and Nelson in several ways. The whole process has taken only minutes instead of months, so it is viewed as a temporary departure from Felix's permanent norm rather than a progression of temporary norms over an extended period. Also it is the result of a deliberately undertaken activity, not the result of misfortune followed by a natural progression that will happen, given time, provided nothing untoward occurs to block the process.

One word of warning. Meditation should be learned under instruction from an experienced teacher who will know what to do if there is a problem. The danger is that, as one ascends the Scale, at some point there may be a drag across to its opposite caused by some trauma or some programme buried in the unconscious of which one is normally unaware. For example there may be a buried fear of losing control which would kick in at +4 or +5, inhibiting transcendence of the ego and possibly sending that person across to the opposite in -4:Self-Abasement or -5:Despair. For most people this will not happen, but for the unlucky few this could be a stumbling block.

Summary

1.   When changing mood it is usual to move one step at a time, up or down or across to the opposite.

2.   An exception is when experiencing something unexpected such as a sudden trauma or sudden major insight. The former immediately places one low on the ladder and the latter immediately places one in a category with a high positive number.

3.   Going downhill is easy, going uphill is usually slower.

4.   Going from a positive to its negative opposite is easy. Going in the other direction, from a negative to its positive opposite, becomes less likely as the number increases. In other words -1 to +1 easy, but from -6 straight into +6 unlikely.

CHAPTER 38

ONE UP

Now we come to a really sneaky mechanism called 'One Up' which has the power to push a person down-scale in an instant.

Previous chapters have considered people responding to situations and then returning to their personal norms when those situations are over. Now it is time to consider more complex interactions. We respond to each other. Interaction is dynamic. One person's reaction can trigger another's which in turn affects the first person, and so on, giving a more fluid picture.

As well as just simply reacting to each other we can go even further by deliberately setting out to cause certain reactions in others. A manipulative person is able to calm people, motivate them, anger them, destroy their self-esteem, and persuade them to engage in actions they would otherwise not have chosen. This is done quite deliberately. Then there are other individuals whose customary behaviour has predictable effects on those around them without their trying, or even intending, those effects. For instance a person who seems not to care tends to annoy, while a cheerful, generous person tends to lift the spirits of those around.

This indicates there must be patterns of interaction regardless of whether the instigators are conscious of them or intend the reactions they produce.

One such pattern is 'One Up'. It occurs when someone is exactly one step above another on the Scale. The effect is to push the second person down a step. The emphasis is on *exactly* one step up as someone two steps higher does not have the same effect. *When A perceives B to be exactly one step up, this pushes A down a step.* For this to make sense it is important to remember that on the right-hand side of Chart 2 'up' goes in the direction from 0 to +6.

This mechanism is a manipulators' weapon since it enables them to wrap others around their little fingers. Victims find it difficult to resist because they are caught up in it before realising what has happened. Anyone who has been a victim of this technique should seriously consider avoiding all future contact with the perpetrator because you never know when he/she will use it again. The technique is so effective that being forewarned is not necessarily the same as being fore-armed.

In all diagrams a downward-pointing arrow ↓ will indicate the effect of the One Up mechanism.

Example 1

Romeo and Bella work together in the same factory and get on together as workmates. Bella realises that he has fallen in love with her but does not feel the same about him and wonders how to deal with this situation.

Initially they are both in +2:Co-operation since they are workmates. But Romeo goes up into +3:Participation as he falls in love. He is now one step up on her, which pushes her down-scale into +1:Exploration, wondering how to deal with him.

DIAGRAM 13
Workmates

Bella   **Romeo**

+2: Co-operation (workmate) . . . . +2: Co-operation (workmate)
↓ . . . . +3: Participation (in love)
+1: Exploration (how to deal with him)

R   +3: Participation

B   +2: Co-operation

+1: Exploration

Example 2

Businessman Sam's secretary is away on holiday and has been replaced by a temp, Delilah, who does not seem up to the job. While she is busy filing her nails he hands her some papers and asks for them to be dealt with as quickly as possible. She replies 'OK' but continues with her manicure. This angers Sam who raises his voice, evoking the response: 'There is no need to shout. I heard you the first time.' Sam is nonplussed. He is not used to this kind of behaviour from an employee.

Sam initiated the interaction by giving Delilah a simple instruction, locating him in -1:Self-Assertion. But she continues filing her nails. In spite of having said 'OK' this appears to her boss as an absence of response on her part, so he perceives her as being at 0:Neutrality which is exactly one step up on him and pushes him down one into -2:Attack. Delilah perceives this as bad manners and tells him not to shout. She is in -1:Self-Assertion which is one up on Sam's new position and pushes him down yet another step into -3:Retreat as he becomes nonplussed. She has pursued him and pushed him down twice.

This is all very unwise on her part because as soon as he recovers and is back in his own personal norm of -1:Self-Assertion, she will be sacked.

DIAGRAM 14
The Boss And A Temp

Sam	His Perception of Delilah	Delilah
-1: Self-Assertion (instructs)	. . . .	-1: Self-Assertion
↓ . . . . 0: Neutrality (no response)		
-2: Attack (anger)		
↓ . . . . -1: Self-Assertion ('Don't shout')	-1: Self-Assertion
-3: Retreat (nonplussed)		

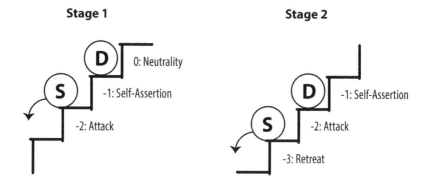

Stage 1

Stage 2

Delilah has actually been in -1:Self-Assertion all the time. The problem here arises from the fact that they both have their personal norms in Self-Assertion which is bound to lead to conflict.

Example 3

Tristan is the four-year-old son of a single mother. One day Tristan is walking along the top of a low garden wall and falls off onto the path below, grazing his hands and knees. These hurt and he cries, attracting his mother's attention. Through the kitchen window Mother sees what has happened and rushes to the open door shouting: 'I told you not to walk on the wall!' Then she goes back into the kitchen to attend to a pot that is beginning to boil over while Tristan remains on the ground, crying. He feels alone and helpless. Eventually Mother does come out to comfort him.

What are the patterns here? When Tristan first hurts himself his attention is focussed entirely on his own pain and is therefore with-

DIAGRAM 15
Tristan Falls Off A Wall

Tristan	His Perception of Mother
-3: Retreat (focused on pain)	
↓	-2: Attack (shouts criticism)
-4: Self-Abasement (all my fault)	
↓	-3: Retreat (she goes indoors)
-5: Despair (alone, helpless)	

drawn from the environment and all else, which puts him into -3: Retreat. Mother goes into -2:Attack as she shouts criticism, which is exactly one step up on Tristan and pushes him down into -4:Self-Abasement – it is all his fault because his mother has just told him so. Instead of picking him up and cuddling him she now goes back into the kitchen. From Tristan's viewpoint this places her in -3:Retreat, exactly one-up on him yet again. So he is pushed down one further step into -5: Despair, feeling alone and helpless.

Example 4

The following imaginary scenario is perhaps somewhat contrived but nevertheless is not far from what can happen in reality.

Rosemary and Basil are in a warm embrace when the telephone rings. They glance at each other with mutual recognition that the interruption will be only temporary. Basil answers the call and learns there is a problem at work. He asks questions to ascertain the exact nature of the problem and whether it requires his attention. After a brief hesitation he agrees to go in to the office straight away, and tells Rosemary. She has not been privy to the telephone conversation so this is a sudden disappointment and she becomes angry. 'Which is more important, your work or me?'

'Rosemary, I am sorry about this, but I must go in to deal with the situation myself.' He explains to her exactly what is wrong and adds that he knows she is a reasonable person and will understand why he has to go. Rosemary has a hang-up about being regarded as lacking in reason and this ploy has the effect of silencing her completely. Her failure to say 'Yes, of course I understand; you must go', leads him to accuse her of sulking whereupon she bursts into tears. In exasperation Basil storms out of the house. Now alone, she feels utterly abandoned and cries her heart out as her world appears to have fallen apart.

What can we make of this scenario in terms of the Scale? In Phase 1 Rosemary and Basil start off in +3:Participation as they embrace. The unexpected ringing of the telephone jerks them both down into +2:Co-operation as they exchange mutual glances. Rosemary now stays in that frame of mind while Basil goes steadily down-scale through +1:Exploration (discovering the problem) and 0:Neutrality (the brief hesitation) into -1:Self-Assertion (he decides to go in to work to sort it out). This has been a steady step-by-step descent.

On being informed of his decision, the disappointment sends Rosemary, who had remained in +2:Co-operation, into its opposite, -2:Attack as she accuses him of putting his work before her.

We now come to Phase 2. At this point Rosemary is exactly one down on Basil so the One Up mechanism comes into play. His calm explanation at -1:Self-Assertion pushes the angry Rosemary from -2:Attack into silence at -3:Retreat. However this lack of response feels to Basil like 0:Neutrality so he gets pushed down from -1:Self-Assertion into -2:Attack, which is once again exactly one-up on Rosemary who promptly bursts into tears at -4:Self-Abasement. On storming out Basil's action is at -3:Retreat leaving her now alone. Thus from her point of view he is one-up yet again and she sinks further down-scale into -5:Despair.

DIAGRAM 16
Basil And Rosemary

Basil	Basil's perception of Rosemary	Rosemary
Phase 1		
+3:Participation (embrace)	+3:Participation	+3:Participation
+2:Co-operation (mutual glance)	+2:Co-operation	+2:Co-operation
+1:Exploration (why the call?)		
0:Neutrality (hesitation)		
-1:Self-Assertion (decision)		
-1:Self-Assertion (informs Rosemary)		
	. . . .	-2: Attack (accuses him)
Phase 2	. . . .	-2: Attack (accuses him)
-1: Self-Assertion (explains)	. . . . ↓	
		-3: Retreat (silence)
↓	0: Neutrality (silence)	
-2: Attack (accuses her)	. . . . ↓	
		-4: Self-Abasement (tears)
-3: Retreat (storms out)	. . . . ↓	
		-5: Despair (abandoned)

Could similar misunderstandings be avoided in the future by using the Scale of Responses? A couples' counsellor would first explain to Basil and Rosemary the patterns they had followed in this drama, and would then discuss whether these were regular patterns in their relationship. Possible alternative responses would be explored together with encouragement to try practising those new responses whenever a similar situation arose.

At first it is likely that they will succeed in being able to understand the dynamics of their interactions only after the events rather than during them. However with growing understanding hopefully they will eventually reach a point at which the recognition occurs within a situation, enabling them to modify their responses at the time and thereby subvert the tendency to go steadily down-scale while winding each other up.

CHAPTER 39

THE KNIGHT'S MOVE, CONTAINMENT

Often situations arise in a relationship in which negative emotions are flying around and one wishes to be able to contain this negativity and prevent it from escalating in a harmful way. This is where the Knight's Move comes in useful.

Example 1

Take the case of four-year-old Tristan (Example 3 in the previous chapter). He has fallen from a low wall and grazed his hands and knees. He sits there crying. What he wants and needs is for his mother to come and give him a cuddle to make it all better.

Tristan's concentration on his own pain was a withdrawal from the environment which placed him in -3:Retreat. What he wanted was for Mum to be the all-healing archetypal Mother who would cuddle him and make everything all right. He wanted her to be the one who can control and cope with the situation (Chart 3). In other words he wanted her to be in +4:Generativity which would have contained his pain and turned the situation into one which was manageable.

DIAGRAM 17
Tristan Comforted

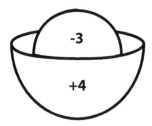

From +4 (archetypal Mother in Generativity) to -3 (Tristan in Retreat) is across to the opposite and then one step up. This 'one step across and one step up' is called the 'Knight's Move' or 'containment'. Yes, I know that in the game of chess a knight's move involves one step one way and TWO steps in the perpendicular direction, but this is what Marshall chose to call it and that name has stuck.

What we have here is a technique for containing negative emotion. *The Knight's Move: A person or overall situation on the plus side of the Scale, can contain a response on the minus side provided it is one step up on the opposite. (n+1) can contain (–n).*

Example 2

Two friends are playing chess. Each is determined to beat the other, so they are both in -2:Attack. But this situation is embedded in a game in which they are both willing participants and enjoy a close and amicable relationship (+3:Participation). This makes the attack situation acceptable and not a threat. -2:Attack is contained within +3: Participation.

DIAGRAM 18
Chess Game

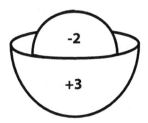

Example 3

In a work situation the foreman gives orders to his men. Provided these orders are given in a spirit of -1:Self-Assertion and not as a fault-finding exercise which would be in -2:Attack, then the workforce accept the situation as being appropriate. They co-operate. In otherwords -1:Self-Assertion is contained within an overall situation of +2:Co-operation.

DIAGRAM 19
Foreman

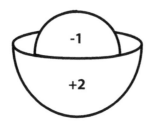

Example 4

The psychological benefits of the Catholic confessional might be explained, at least in part, as the containment of guilt at -4:Self-Abasement within the embrace of Divine acceptance at +5:Emancipation.

DIAGRAM 20
Confessional

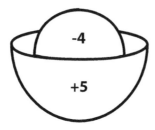

The Knight's Move is a useful tool in the counsellor's or psychotherapist's armoury since frequently there is a need to contain a client's negativity. However in order to be able to do this therapists need to be in good psychological shape and able to move up and down the Scale on the plus side as required. They must be able to go into, or appear to go into, any state up as far as the ego-transcendent state of +6:Transpersonalization. Hence the need for them to have undergone extensive therapy themselves to remove their own potential stumbling blocks.

There is no +7 on the Scale. This makes the Knight's Move inoperable when a client is in the extreme disintegrated state of -6: Depersonalization.

CHAPTER 40

SUBPERSONALITIES

We all adapt our behaviour according to the situation in which we find ourselves. This may just involve a change in mood, which has been discussed in previous chapters, but it might also produce an apparent change in personality. We are complex creatures and our personalities have many different facets.

Inside each of us are a number of different subpersonalities.[1] They are like a cast of different characters in the theatre of the person that each one of us happens to be. Some may appear frequently, others rarely, and some change over time as we become older and (hopefully) wiser.

Before going any further let me make it absolutely clear that this has nothing whatever to do with split personalities which constitute a pathological state of mind. Subpersonalities are normal. We all have them. In fact we have quite a lot of them.

For example consider the dad who is Mr Fix-It when mending his son's broken toys, Hail-Fellow-Well-Met when with friends in the local pub, and Raging Bull to his employees. And this will not be all. He is likely to have quite a few more characters tucked away in the theatre of his psyche.

Each subpersonality behaves as if it were a complete personality in its own right. It has its own role, its own likes and dislikes, its own goals. It is even possible for someone to have two subpersonalities which disagree with each other producing what feels like an inner traffic jam. An example is the dilemma created when person A has to decide whether or not to impart bad news to person B who is likely to become upset. One part of A considers that B has a right to know, while another part of A hates upsetting people.

My own current cast of characters include Teacher, Sort It, and Little Old Lady, amongst others. Teacher is easy to explain since teaching was my main career, but in fact it goes back further, to the days when I used to line up all my dolls and soft toys in front of a small blackboard. This part of me wants to carry on teaching and correcting people, a trait which can cause problems if not carefully checked.

Sort It also goes back a long way. This is that part of me that mends things that are broken or torn, and that looks for ways to calm things down when friends are in dispute.

Little Old Lady is a member of the cast only recently discovered. My mobility scooter is a joy to ride at 8 mph when on the road, there is the ready excuse of old age when a familiar name escapes me, and if I complain about an uncomfortable chair solicitous friends and relatives go out of their way to find another.

A person's subpersonalities can interact with each other in just the same ways that preceding chapters have described for interactions between people. Each has its norm, and when two come into co-operation or conflict then One Up and The Knight's Move apply. The following two examples are from my own experience.

Example 1

Recently I felt that the government were not dealing correctly with a certain important issue and that their solutions would only make matters worse. So I decided to write to our local member of parliament. That was Teacher being critical, wanting to correct an error. But Little Old Lady felt weary and lacked energy for the task, so writing the letter was put off for another day.

DIAGRAM 21
Teacher And Little Old Lady

Teacher	Little Old Lady
-1: Self-Assertion (norm)	
-2: Attack (criticism)	
↓ .... -1: Self-Assertion (need to relax)	
-3: Retreat (postpones action)	

Teacher's norm is -1:Self-Assertion, but she had gone down into -2:Attack when forming the intention to send a letter of criticism. But Little Old Lady did not feel so inclined and asserted her lack of energy as an excuse for not becoming involved. This happened to be at -1:Self-Assertion, one up on Teacher who was currently at -2:Attack. The One Up mechanism came into play, pushing Teacher down a step into -3:Retreat as she postponed writing the letter.

Actually it never did get written.

Example 2

My tendency to be overweight is due to a subpersonality called Indulgence while advice about restraint and exercise comes from Sensible. Their norms are both at -1:Self-Assertion which puts them into direct conflict. Frequently Indulgent prevails and Sensible goes into disapproval, a mild form of -2:Attack. But this means that Indulgent is now one up on Sensible which pushes the latter down one more step into silent surrender at -3:Retreat. Indulgent has won the battle.

DIAGRAM 22
Indulgent And Sensible

Indulgent	Sensible
-1: Self-Assertion	-1: Self-Assertion (restraint)
	-2: Attack (critical)
-1: Self-Assertion . . . . ↓	
	-3: Retreat (surrender)

Each individual's cast of subpersonalities is unique to that person, and the variety that can occur is unlimited. To name just a few possibilities there could be: Sage, Campaigner, Practical Joker, Clown, Do Good, Alice (dreams and fantasises), Steam Kettle, Doormat, Smoke Screen (secretive), Peacock, Night Owl, and so on. The possibilities are endless.

The theory of subpersonalities can be complex, and attempts to identify one's own ideally require a suitably qualified supervisor. This is usually carried out in workshops which are run by professionals.

Some books on the subject give programmes of exercises based on imagery which are intended to reveal one's subpersonalities, but it is not advisable to practise these on one's own because any digging into the unconscious has the capability of bringing to the surface something which is difficult to handle, let alone understand.

For an introduction to the theory and identification of subpersonalities one cannot do better than refer to the book which describes the
workshops of the Centre for Transpersonal Psychology [1]. These were
an integral part of the training course for transpersonal psychotherapists
run by the pioneering couple Ian Gordon-Brown and Barbara Somers
from the 1970's to the 1990's in London.

CHAPTER 41

EXAMPLES FOR ANALYSIS

The reader is invited to consider the following scenarios and to place their participants' responses on the Scale which is shown in Chart 2. Suggested answers can be found in the next chapter.

It may be helpful to refer to the expanded Scale of Chart 4 in order to clarify the variety of responses and attitudes which each of the thirteen steps contains. However Chart 2 remains the basis for any analysis.

Example 1
Can you locate the norm for each of the following?
a) Ash has a keen, enquiring mind and has chosen a career which suits him admirably, namely that of a research scientist. This sometimes exasperates his wife because he is forever asking her where, how and why instead of just accepting her conversational titbits. His friends and colleagues find him easy to get on with though there is no depth in these relationships. He seems to have no ability to relate to others' feelings, living very much in his head. In any disagreement he expresses his own point of view as if he is an authority on the subject, totally regardless of whether or not he is really clued up on the subject.
b) Rowan is known to his friends as opinionated, prejudiced and rigid in his views. He shows no interest in the concerns of others and is easily provoked. At home he is dictatorial and has been known to hit his wife. When something happens which could be to his advantage he milks it to its full extent.
c) Olive recently married and is very happy. That is until one day she discovers the scent of another woman's perfume on her husband's shirt. Fear of losing him overcomes her.

Example 2
When carrying out her weekly shop in the supermarket Jasmine

carefully examines the items before deciding what to buy.

Example 3

In the original Star Trek series Dr McCoy (the Emotions Man) frequently asserts the justifiability, indeed the desirability, of having emotions and expressing them. He fails to make an impression on Mr Spock (the Mind Man) who comes across to McCoy as cold and non-reactive. This exasperates McCoy.

Example 4

A small child shouts 'I hate you!' to his mother and then runs out of the room banging the door en route. The wise mother knows the child is just having a tantrum and does not really mean it. They have a good loving relationship.

Example 5

It is the very first day for five-year-olds to go to school. Daisy is looking forward to it. She anticipates meeting new friends and having new experiences, and she is not disappointed as the day goes by. On the other hand Violet is a shy child who depends on her mother. The thought of having to spend much of the day without mother and in the company of strangers, fills her with apprehension and fear. As the day passes she becomes more and more unhappy.

Example 6

A man is threatened by a mugger brandishing a knife. Salvador rushes to the rescue and the mugger runs away.

Example 7

A thief accosts an old lady in the street and demands she hand over her money. She gives him her purse and he runs off.

Example 8

Fourteen-year-olds Holly and Ivy are best friends. They do everything together to the extent that their schoolmates describe them as living in each others' pockets. Holly happens to be good at art and decides to join a local art club, and of course Ivy goes too because they are inseparable.

But it is not really Ivy's cup of tea and she begins to wonder why she is there at all. She is just not interested and eventually says so to her friend. Up to this point Holly has been blissfully unaware of her friend's unease and becomes angry that nothing was said about it before. Ivy announces that she will cease attending the club and that Holly will have to continue on her own. This leaves Holly speechless. Unfortunately Ivy thinks that Holly's silence is a sign of not caring, and explodes in anger, whereupon Holly feels guilty and apologises profusely for failing to notice how her best friend felt. This takes the wind out of Ivy's sails because such an apology has never happened before, and she too becomes apologetic. At this point both friends break into tears, hug and make up.

Example 9

Crystal is in the kitchen where she slips and bangs her head as she falls. Rock hears her cry and comes rushing into the room where he finds her unconscious on the floor. He is not easily flustered so he calmly feels her pulse, which is beating. He must do something. But what? Then he takes himself in hand and telephones for an ambulance. He begins to wonder what on earth she was doing to get into this position – probably something stupid. When the ambulance arrives he is relieved and does everything the medics ask him to do.

Example 10

Jasper and Beryl are married. They are not in love but manage to get on with each other satisfactorily. One day Beryl receives notification that she has won a prestigious award. Proudly she tells Jasper who reacts with fury. She is non-plussed. Later she considers what happened and comes to the conclusion he is jealous. Then she realizes that this is not the first instance, because he has regularly prevented her from engaging in activities that she would have enjoyed. So from now on she pretends that she wants the opposite of what she really desires, and that way she gets what she actually wants.

Example 11

Perdita is homeless and feeling suicidal. A priest talks to her about God and Jesus. This is the first time that Perdita has really attended to this message and the idea of a divine Saviour gets through to her. She feels unworthy but the priest assures her that Jesus is caring and regards no-one as beyond redemption.

Example 12

Leo is the leader of a political party. He is a born leader, supported by most of his members, with a way of silencing any critics. After the party's defeat in an election he loses much of their support and holds himself responsible. He feels no longer in contact with his party and announces his resignation. He wishes to spend more time with his family who remain supportive.

Example 13

During the weigh-in before an important match it is customary for both boxers to boast about how they will win over their opponent. This is done to psych themselves up for the fight, during which they go all out to win.

Example 14

In Milgram's famous experiment to demonstrate obedience to authority[1], volunteers were paired off with a person whose role was to answer questions, and then each volunteer was required to assume the role of teacher asking questions and administer ever-increasing electric shocks if the partner gave a wrong answer. What they did not know was that the partners were actors and the shocks did not exist. The following scenario is adapted from the archive tapes.[2]

A certain 'teacher' went along with the experiment until he became disturbed by his partner's reactions and condemned the experiment. The experimenter urged him to continue saying that the experiment must go on. The 'teacher' was silenced and resumed the experiment, but soon became disturbed again. The experimenter again urged compliance but this time the 'teacher' refused to continue.

Example 15

In prison is a convict who is aggressive and violent and whom the other prisoners respect as the leader of a bullying gang. A newcomer to his gang addresses him as 'brother'. For him this is a new experience and there develops a friendship of mutual respect. He adopts the newcomer's ideology and becomes radicalised.

Example 16

As a child Ernest's father used to berate him for daydreaming which made him feel guilty. As a result in adulthood Ernest is diligent and hard-working. He decides to attend a meditation class. Initially the practice goes well, but as soon as he reaches the state of feeling unencumbered by everyday cares and tasks, guilt sets in and he cannot continue.

CHAPTER 42

ANALYSES

This chapter contains my own take on the situations described in the previous chapter. This is not an exact science and alternative interpretations may be possible.

ℵ) — ℭ

1. a) Ash's career choice and the way in which he interacts with his wife indicate a personal norm at +1:Exploration. In communication with others he is co-operative but neutral with regard to their feelings, and is self-assertive during any dispute. From his norm these are moves one up, one down, and across to the opposite, respectively.

DIAGRAM 23
Ash's Norm

0: Neutrality (no interest)

-1: Self-Assertion (authoritative) . . . . +1: Exploration (Ash's norm)

+2: Co-operation (friends)

b) Because Rowan is opinionated and rigid in his views, this suggests a personal norm at -1:Self-Assertion. His lack of interest in others is at Neutrality, and his behaviour at home at Attack. It is only when there is something to his advantage that he goes into Exploration which is the opposite to his norm.

DIAGRAM 24
Rowan's Norm

0: Neutrality (no interest)

-1: Self Assertion (Rowan's norm) . . . . +1: Exploration (to his advantage)

-2: Attack (beats wife)

c) Because she is a newly-wed it is safe to assume that her norm is in +3:Participation rather than +2:Co-operation. In Participation one's whole being is involved and there is a sense of bonding, whereas +2:Co-operation is more like fulfilment of a contract. This is confirmed by her sudden switch to suspicion and fear which are in -3:Retreat and the opposite to her norm in +3.

DIAGRAM 25
Olive's Norm

-3: Retreat (fear) . . . .   +3: Participation (Olive's norm)

ℰꙮ — ℭꙮ

2. Jasmine examines the items in +1:Exploration and then goes into -1:Self-Assertion on deciding what to purchase. Shopping involves repeated fluctuations between these two opposites.

DIAGRAM 26
Shopping

-1: Self-Assertion (decisions) . . . .   +1: Exploration (examines items)

ℰꙮ — ℭꙮ

3. McCoy, asserting his point of view, is at -1:Self-Assertion. Spock appears to be non-reactive which puts him at 0:Neutrality in the eyes of McCoy. This is one up and pushes McCoy down into exasperation at -2:Attack.

DIAGRAM 27
Star Trek

McCoy   **His Perception of Spock**

-1: Self-Assertion . . . .
↓ . . . . 0: Neutrality
-2: Attack . . . .

ℰꙮ — ℭꙮ

4. The child's shout is in -2:Attack which immediately goes down into -3:Retreat as he runs out of the room. But -3:Retreat is contained by +4: Generativity, the mother's understanding and the relationship they share.

DIAGRAM 28
Mother And Child

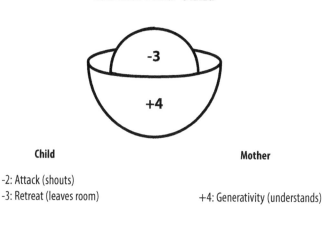

Child	Mother
-2: Attack (shouts)	
-3: Retreat (leaves room)	+4: Generativity (understands)

ℰ — ℛ

5. Daisy's anticipation is trusting and is located in +3:Participation. As the day goes by she may well experience joy and enthusiasm in +4: Generativity. Certainly there will be times when she explores the situation (+1:Exploration), for example when meeting other children for the first time, and she co-operates with the teacher's instructions (+2:Co-operation).

DIAGRAM 29
First Day At School

Daisy	Violet
+1: Exploration (new experiences)	
+2: Co-operation (fitting in)	
+3: Participation (trusting)	-3: Retreat (fear)
+4: Generativity (joy, enthusiasm)	-4: Self-Abasement (cannot cope)
	-5: Despair

Violet is naturally shy, which is at -3:Retreat. Normally this is contained by mother at +4:Generativity (the Knight's move) but today she approaches her time at school with trepidation (-3:Retreat). During the day she becomes more unhappy as she goes down into -4:Self-Abasement (cannot cope) and possibly -5:Despair.

℘ — ℭ

6. Threatening someone with a knife is undoubtedly at -2:Attack. Salvador rushes in to do something about it. He is endeavouring to change the situation in some way so he is on the minus side of the Scale, in -1:Self-Assertion. This is one-up on the mugger who is pushed down into -3:Retreat as he runs away.

DIAGRAM 30
Salvador

Mugger   **His Perception of Salvador**

-2: Attack (threatens with knife)
↓ ....   -1: Self-Assertion (taking charge)
-3: Retreat (runs away)

Rushing in to help will not always work. It depends on how the mugger perceives this action. If he perceives it as an attack upon himself (-2:Attack) rather than as another person gaining charge of the situation, then the one-up mechanism will not work and Salvador might have come off worst.

℘ — ℭ

7. The thief demands money. He is in -1:Self-Assertion. From his point of view the old lady responds in +2:Co-operation by handing over her purse. Had she hesitated she would have appeared to him to be in 0:Neutrality, which would have been one-up on him and would have pushed him down into -2:Attack. However her apparent response of co-operation contained him and the situation came to an end. True she lost her money, but at the same time the situation was saved from escalating into something more violent.

DIAGRAM 31
Mugging of Old Lady

The thief's perception

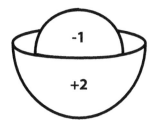

What might have occurred

Thief	His Perception of Her
-1: Self-Assertion (demands)	
↓ .... 0: Neutrality	
-2: Attack	

ℰ𝒪 — 𝒞ℛ

8. The two friends enjoy a bonding relationship which puts their norm in +3:Participation. In attending the art club Ivy is no longer whole-heartedly into their activity together while Holly clearly enjoys it. So Ivy has slipped down into +2:Co-operation while Holly remains at +3, which is exactly one step up on her friend. The one-up mechanism now comes into play and Ivy is pushed down into +1:Exploration, where-upon she questions why she is there.

Ivy soon realises that she is just not interested in the art club and decides to speak about it to her friend. Having explored what is wrong with the situation there is now a need to see that it is put right. She has flipped across from +1 to its opposite in -1:Self-Assertion.

Holly is unaware of what has been going on in her friend's mind so she is still in +3:Participation, enjoying their friendship and the art classes which they attend together. Ivy's revelation comes as a sudden blow. Holly is temporarily speechless which is a flip across from +3 to its opposite in -3:Retreat where she is momentarily stunned. Unfortunately Ivy misinterprets her friend's silence as an indication of not having understood or of being indifferent, and incorrectly perceives

Holly as being in 0:Neutrality. Because Ivy is currently in -1:Self-Assertion, this puts her perception of Holly exactly one step up, which in turn sends Ivy down one step into -2:Attack. She becomes angry.

We now have Holly in -3:Retreat and Ivy in -2:Attack which is one step up on Holly. This in turn pushes Holly down yet another step into -4:Self-Abasement where she feels guilty and apologises for her own failure to be aware of Ivy's feelings. Ivy is taken by surprise and for a moment is at a loss how to respond. This unexpected situation has taken her from -2:Attack into -3:Retreat, temporary disconnection. But she also carries on going down the ladder as she sees herself to blame, and ends up in -4:Self-Abasement where she, too, becomes apologetic.

The two friends are now both in -4:Self-Abasement. Neither is one up on the other and so they no longer have the effect of pushing each other down-scale. They commiserate together and are then able to rise back up-scale to resume their normal relationship in +3:Participation. Their friendship has reached a new understanding.

DIAGRAM 32
Holly And Ivy

Ivy	Ivy's perception of Holly	Holly
+3: Participation	+3: Participation	+3: Participation
+2: Co-operation		
↓	+3: Participation	
+1: Exploration (why am I here?)		
-1: Self-Assertion (speaks up)		
↓	0:Neutrality	-3: Retreat (speechless)
-2: Attack (angry)		↓
. . . .		-4: Self-Abasement (apologetic)
-3: Retreat (nonplussed)		
-4: Self-Abasement (apologetic)		-4: Self-Abasement (apologetic)

This example also illustrates the fact that a minus sign on the chart is not necessarily bad. At the end of this scenario it was the best thing that could have happened when Ivy went into -4:Self-Abasement, for without this they might never have healed their differences.

℘ — ℭ

9. Rock's first reaction is calmly to examine Crystal to find out how bad the situation is, which puts him at +1:Exploration. Then he is determined to do something. He has gone across to the opposite, namely -1:Self-assertion. Back to +1:Exploration as he considers what to do, and again to -1:Self-Assertion when he telephones for an ambulance. Now on his own and waiting for the ambulance to arrive, he goes down another step into -2:Attack as he blames Crystal for her supposed stupidity. The arrival of the ambulance reassures him and he does everything the medics ask, so he has flipped across to the opposite +2:Co-operation.

DIAGRAM 33
Accident Indoors

Rock

+1: Exploration (examines her)
-1: Self-Assertion (must do something)
+1: Exploration (what to do?)
-1: Self-Assertion (telephones for an ambulance)
-2: Attack (blames her stupidity)
+2: Co-operation (does as asked)

This flipping back and forth between +1:Exploration and -1:Self-Assertion is usual when a decision is required. It occurs also in the earlier example about shopping.

ℬ — ℭ

10. Initially Beryl is in +2:Co-operation, her norm in the relationship, and she assumes that so is Jasper. Good news takes her up into a frank sharing with him (+3:Participation) but only to find that he is in -2: Attack, whereupon she flips across to her opposite in -3:Retreat as she is temporarily non-plussed.

Later on, having recovered she goes into +1:Exploration, near to her norm, while trying to understand. When an explanation occurs she takes control of the situation by manipulating him, and is now in -1:Self-Assertion.

Contrary to Beryl's original assumption about their co-operative relationship Jasper had actually been in -1:Self-Assertion all along, as he endeavoured to be the one in control. This had been OK because, by the Knight's Move, his controlling was contained within an overall framework of +2:Co-operation.

After the incident between them he recovered his manipulating norm at -1, not realizing that he was now the one being manipulated.

DIAGRAM 34
Control

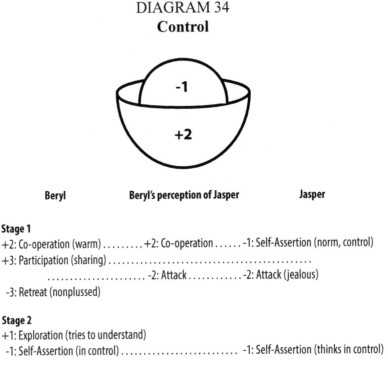

Beryl	Beryl's perception of Jasper	Jasper

Stage 1
+2: Co-operation (warm) . . . . +2: Co-operation . . . . . . -1: Self-Assertion (norm, control)
+3: Participation (sharing) . . . .
. . . . -2: Attack . . . . -2: Attack (jealous)
 -3: Retreat (nonplussed)

Stage 2
+1: Exploration (tries to understand)
 -1: Self-Assertion (in control) . . . . -1: Self-Assertion (thinks in control)

11. Perdita is suicidal and in -5:Despair. She is not in -6:Depersonalization because she still has a sense of her own self and her needs. The priest's message gives her an impression of a divine Saviour who is in +6:Transpersonalization, which contains her. She becomes aware of feeling unworthy, which is an upgrade into -4:Self-Abasement, whereupon the priest's message is now one of divine redemption and total acceptance at +5:Emancipation. Again the Knight's Move contains her. Hopefully her rise up-scale will continue.

DIAGRAM 35
Homeless

Perdita	Her perception of Jesus

-5: Despair (suicidal) . . . .
. . . . +6: Transpersonalization (divine)
-4: Self-Abasement (unworthy) . . . .
. . . . +5: Emancipation (total acceptance)

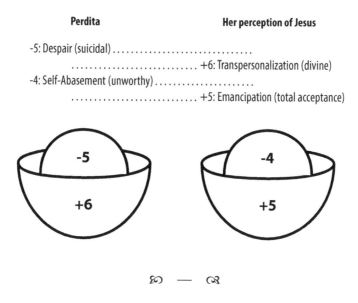

ε◌ — ◌Ͽ

12. Leo is a born leader and his norm is at -1:Self-Assertion. He is supported by most of his members, which is an example of -1:Self-Assertion contained within +2:Co-operation. The few critics who are at -2:Attack are pushed down into silence at -3:Retreat by the fact that he is one-up on them at -1. But when the party is soundly defeated at the election he goes down a step from -1 into -2:Attack when he criticises himself. He sinks down a further step to -3:Retreat when he feels out of touch and eventually resigns, at which point he is supported and contained by his family at +4:Generativity.

With the continued loving support of his family it is likely he will gradually return to his norm of -1:Self-Assertion.

DIAGRAM 36
Party Leader

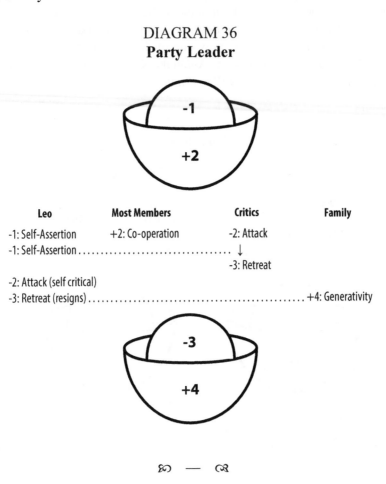

Leo	Most Members	Critics	Family
-1: Self-Assertion	+2: Co-operation	-2: Attack	
-1: Self-Assertion		↓	
		-3: Retreat	
-2: Attack (self critical)			
-3: Retreat (resigns)			+4: Generativity

ဆ — ౧

13. Boasting is an example of -1:Self-Assertion, and because it is practised as part of the pre-match ritual it is acceptable by being contained within +2:Co-operation. During the fight there is an all-out attempt on both sides to win, which puts them both in -2:Attack. However once again there is an overall scenario of being embedded in a match in which they are bonded together in a mutual activity which has rules of engagement which they accept. This implies containment within +3:Participation.

At least this is how it is viewed by the onlookers and it may, or may not, be how the two boxers view the situation. It is possible they have psyched themselves up into a hatred of their respective opponents and are all out to defeat him in an attitude of -2:Attack.

DIAGRAM 37
Boxers

Before the Match

-1: Self-Assertion (boasting
+2: Co-operation (custom)

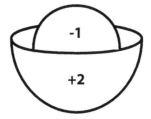

During the Fight

-2: Attack (fighting to win)
+3: Participation (shared rules of engagement)

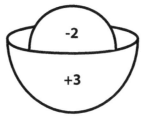

It must be added that I know nothing about boxing or boxers so I may have got this completely wrong.

80 — 03

14. The experimenter was the authority at -1:Self-Assertion through-out. Initially the 'teacher' co-operated. Self-Assertion was accepted and contained within +2:Co-operation.

When the 'teacher' condemned the situation he had switched across to the opposite at -2:Attack. However the experimenter at -1:Self-assertion was now one-up on him and pushed him down into -3:Retreat, where he ceased objecting. He resumed his co-operation.

This exchange occurred a second time, but now his misgivings had more force and his retreat took the form of abandoning the experiment.

DIAGRAM 38
Milgram's Experiment [1]

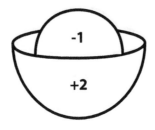

Experimenter	Teacher
-1: Self-Assertion (authority)	+2: Co-operation (experiment)
	-2: Attack (condemns)
-1: Self-Assertion	↓
	-3: Retreat (reduced to silence)
	+2: Co-operation (resumes experiment)
	-2: Attack (stronger objection)
-1: Self-Assertion	↓
	-3: Retreat (discontinues)

ଞ — ଔ

15. The convict's norm is -2:Attack. When leading his gang he may go up into -1:Self-Assertion, contained by the gang in an overall spirit of +2:Co-operation. The newcomer's friendly approach comes across as being in +3:Participation which contains the first man's norm of -2: Attack. This containment facilitates the radicalisation process.[2]

DIAGRAM 39
Convict And Newcomer

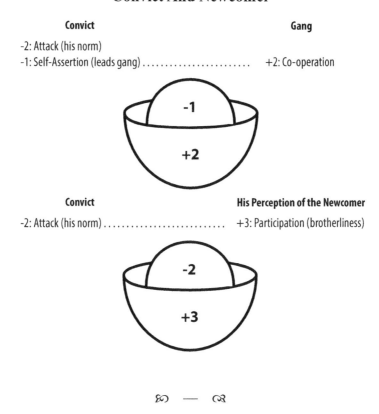

Convict   **Gang**

-2: Attack (his norm)

-1: Self-Assertion (leads gang) . . . .   +2: Co-operation

Convict   **His Perception of the Newcomer**

-2: Attack (his norm) . . . .   +3: Participation (brotherliness)

🙚 — 🙘

16. When Ernest's father berated him at -2:Attack, Ernest flipped
across from happy day-dreaming, +4:Generativity, to its opposite
-4:Self-Abasement, feeling guilty. This establishes in him an unconscious programme[3] of guilt when not getting on with things. Consequently as an adult he is diligent and hard-working which puts his norm
at +2:Co-operation.

The meditation process takes him up step by step to +3:Participation
and then +4:Generativity, at which point the unconscious programme
which originated in his childhood kicks in and he is shot across to the
opposite in -4:Self-Abasement.

DIAGRAM 40
Ernest's Programme

Father   **Ernest as a child**   **Adult Ernest**

+4: Generativity (day dreaming)

-2: Attack (berates Ernest) . . . .

-4: Self-Abasement (guilty)

An unconscious programme has been formed

+2: Co-operation (norm)

+3: Participation (meditating)

+4: Generativity

-4: Self-Abasement

CHAPTER 43

KNOWLEDGE AND WISDOM

A little learning is a dang'rous thing [1]

Now that the reader has the basics for using this Scale, observation in real life will enable its application to more complex and fluid situations rather than the somewhat simplified scenarios that have been encountered as examples in these pages.

Knowledge and understanding of the techniques described in the foregoing chapters will confer power but not necessarily wisdom. Armed with this power one can choose to do good or ill. One can use the skills involved for the benefit of others and to make life more pleasant for all, including oneself, or they can be used for one's own ends.

This distinction applies most particularly to the one-up mechanism. It can be used to gain power over others by manipulation and by pushing them down into emotional and psychological depths which they are unable to control; or knowledge of the technique can be employed to avoid sending others down and to avoid being manipulated oneself.

It is worth bearing in mind that, to a large extent we create our own social environment. For example deceitful people tend to be suspicious that they are surrounded by deceit, bossy persons are likely to be discomforted by the presence of authority, and vicious people frequently meet a sticky end. This same principle can also be true on the positive side of the Scale. Helpful and compassionate folk tend to be helped by their friends when in difficulty. The vibes that we project are reflected back to us.

Much will depend on the degree to which we know ourselves and to what extent unconscious patterns are in control of our responses and motivations.[2] Wisdom comes only with a combination of experience and self-knowledge.

PART 3:

CONCLUSION

CHAPTER 44

CONTINUUM

There have been many attempts to categorise the different aspects of any human being: body-soul-spirit (early western), body-mind-spirit (eastern yoga), body-mind-emotions-spirit (recent western). Although the bit in the middle has varied because of different concepts and definitions related to the psyche, they are all clear that our components include the physical and the spiritual. Moreover in these descriptions the various aspects remain separate and distinct although interacting.

What these pages have tried to show is that they are not separate and distinct but merge in a continuum which is related to evolution.

Part 1 dealt with motivating needs ranging from the physiological, through the emotional and social, to the spiritual, in a system which forms a seamless whole.

Part 2 described our moods and responses from the personal, through the interpersonal or social, to the transpersonal or spiritual, again forming a seamless whole. It might seem that the physiological aspect is missing from this second system, but that is not so. Every response is accompanied by some kind of physiological change, whether it be in blood pressure, heart rate, or signals in the brain and the flow of chemicals through the body. In fact some of these changes have acquired their own popular names such as 'the fight or flight response' and 'the relaxation response'.[1]

While the continuum in Part 1 is underpinned by evolution, the system in Part 2 is underpinned by our physiology, which in turn is biological and the result of evolution.

It has been shown that these two systems, the Motivation Hierarchy and the Scale of Responses, represent patterns which are inherent in every human being regardless of the fact that, due to differing personal circumstances, many individuals do not actually realize the full spectra during their lifetimes. Nevertheless the potential is there.

This confirms that these two systems are biologically-rooted and somehow embedded in our genes, which brings us to the evolutionary continuum. How do our motivating needs and responses compare with those of other species? What are their psyches like? Until people like Dian Fossey[2] and David Attenborough[3] began their work these questions were not even asked.

Scientists can stick electrodes onto the scalps of monkeys to observe brain function, but that is a far cry from being able to understand their minds. Mammals like dolphins whose natural environment is water, cannot be subjected even to this minimal attempt at understanding. What little knowledge we have of the minds of other creatures is from direct experience, and that is subject to the vagaries of personal interpretation.

Our best chance is with our pet dogs with whom we manage to set up a mutual rapport. Those of us who are responsible owners try to give them everything they need to be healthy and happy and to be fully who they are according to their canine natures. However although it is our motivation that they should self-actualize it does not follow that they also have that ambition. Moreover we do not attribute to them the ability to be motivated by ideals. What we can say is that they are capable of being motivated by the need to esteem their owner, their pack leader. In terms of the Motivation Hierarchy it is suggested that they have all the levels up to and including Esteem, and maybe also Self-Actualization.

Dogs are able to feel grief and joy but there is no indication that they can experience the extreme states of consciousness allocated to ±6 on the Scale of Responses. We can agree that their Scale of Responses includes -4:Self-Abasement and +4:Generativity. As for -5:Despair it is my opinion that dogs that are seriously ill-treated go into this state, which implies that the canine psyche also has the potential to experience +5:Emancipation. However we can probably all agree that they do not have the ability to experience -6:Depersonalization and +6:Transpersonalization.

So, although we appear to share much of these two systems with our pets, it is in our spiritual aspects that we have evolved something extra.

What about dolphins? As already mentioned the fact that they inhabit a watery environment mean that we cannot even examine their brains in action. As far as dolphins in the wild are concerned all we have are anecdotes. When it comes to members of their species in captivity, at least there are humans who have established some kind of rapport. The problem is that captive dolphins are no longer free to be who they are, their environment does not have the variety of the open sea, they cannot exercise their navigational skills and their instinct to roam the oceans, and their social life is severely restricted.

We do know that they are highly intelligent with a complex language, and in the wild have a complex social life. It is not unreasonable to think that their natural motivating needs include Self-Actualization. Do they also include Intrinsic Values? Anecdotes suggest they can feel compassion for another species and that is certainly a value. But when it comes to the Scale of Responses our inability to understand their language and gestures makes it impossible even to speculate about whether the Scale applies to them at all. It is only the fact that they are mammals which makes us think that they do share at least some of the Scale with us if not all of it.

This brings us back to the fact that the Motivation Hierarchy and the Scale of Responses both arose ultimately from the process of evolution. Life in the earliest organisms evolved into the life of all the plants and creatures around us as well as the life in ourselves. We share elements of our DNA. The whole of life is a continuum.

Provided the human race does not destroy that life with pollution, destruction of habitats, and depletion of resources, all of which are exacerbated by over-population, then we can expect evolution to continue into the future. Nature has always had ways of restoring balance so perhaps we can expect a severe reduction in the world's human population at some point in the future. Whether that will be brought about by wars, disease or by the exercise of plain common sense, who knows?

Assuming that we survive into the future, in what way will we continue to evolve? Will *homo sapiens* become *homo transcendens* or *homo something else*? Will additional levels be added to the Motivation Hierarchy and the Scale of Responses? Not only is it impossible for us to predict, it is also impossible for us to imagine or comprehend what those extra levels might be, in just the same way that a chimpanzee cannot comprehend Intrinsic Values or Transpersonalization.

What we are justified in assuming is that the current aspects of the continuum will not be eliminated but will be built upon by adding yet more levels and retaining the continuity of an integrated set of systems.

ADDENDA

APPENDIX

This paper was first published by the British Psychological Society in December 2014 in the monthly journal The Psychologist, vol.27, no.12, pages 982-983. It is an account of Maslow's reasons for adding Intrinsic Values to his already widely published Hierarchy of Needs which had Self-Actualization at the top.

MASLOW'S HIERARCHY OF NEEDS – THE SIXTH LEVEL
by **Hazel Skelsey Guest**

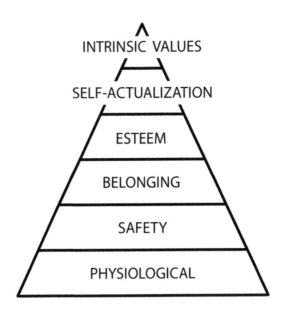

Cambridge University has a residential adult education centre in the delightful Madingley Hall. Some time ago I ran a weekend course there on 'The Life and Work of Abraham Maslow' and among the end-of-course essays I was surprised to find that two students reproduced the Hierarchy of Needs with only five levels – physiological, safety, belonging, esteem, and self-actualization. This was in spite of the fact that I had spent one and a half hours on the sixth level – intrinsic values – which Maslow added to his list of motivational needs shortly before his death. It seemed that these students had previously been taught that there are five basic motivations, with self-actualization at the top, and as far as they were concerned nothing I had said would change that. What was going on?

The clue was in the fact that the students fell into two distinct groups. There were those who came from a background in humanistic or transpersonal psychology, and were either already familiar with the sixth motivation or ready to accept it. The other group had a background in the practical application of motivation theory to the world of business and management, and to them self-actualization was the ultimate goal and the sixth level was completely new. The first group were ignorant of Maslow's extensive practical work in applying his theories to the workplace and the boardroom, while the second group had never heard of his theoretical work on self-actualizers, what motivates them, peak experiences or humanistic and transpersonal psychology.

How had this dichotomy between two different branches of psychology come about? The answer is historical.

Abraham Maslow (1908-1970), some time President of the American Psychological Association, is best known for his work on human motivation and in particular for his Hierarchy of Needs, which was first defined in a paper of 1943. This 1943 paper subsequently became a standard feature in the practical application of motivation theory in business and management, and it has been reproduced in at least 22 different books and journals (Maslow, 1971/1976 pp379-380).

Five basic needs are defined, all of which he considered to be hard-wired into the human species. They are arranged hierarchically, with self-actualization referring to:

> ...people's desire for self-fulfillment, namely, the tendency for them to become actualized in what they are potentially. This tendency might be phrased as the desire to become more and more what

one idiosyncratically is, to become everything that one is capable of becoming.

(Maslow, 1943; 1954/1987 p 22)

Maslow's 1943 paper mentions cognitive needs such as the desire to know and to understand, and also aesthetics, but does not place them within the hierarchy of five. In other words Maslow recognised, even at this early stage, that his list was incomplete. In spite of this reservation it has been widely reproduced as a complete theory, on the way acquiring its own pictorial representation in the form of a triangle or pyramid which is reproduced in countless publications.

Because the five needs are latently or actively present in all members of the human species, they are described as being 'biologically rooted'. This is a key theme throughout Maslow's work. He is dealing with the characteristics of a particular species, some of which may be shared with other species, but nevertheless he avoids extrapolating from one species to another.

The higher need is a later phyletic or evolutionary development. We share the need for food with all living things, the need for love with (perhaps) the higher apes, the need for self-actualization with nobody. The higher the need the more specifically human it is.

(Maslow, 1954/1987 p57).

Following the 1943 paper Maslow's work took two distinct directions. One was the practical application of his theories to the workplace. This involved detailed observation of working practices in various organisations with a view to improving motivation, and with this work came international recognition. An example is the journal he kept while at Non-Linear Systems in Del Mar, California in the summer of 1962, which was republished recently as *Maslow On Management* (1998).

The other strand to his work involved a study of those people who could be considered to be self-actualizers: those who have achieved, or are achieving, their full potential as individuals (Maslow 1962/1968). The obvious question he asked was: If someone is already self-actualizing, what then motivates that person? In seeking an answer he came up with motivation by intrinsic values such as 'truth, goodness, beauty, perfection, excellence, simplicity, elegance, and so on' (Maslow, 1969 p4), in other words values that transcend the individual's personal self-interests and for which he coined the term 'B-values'. This is in contrast to the other five motivational levels, all of which involve self-interest in some form or other. In turn this led to concepts such as ego-transcendence and peak-experiences (Maslow, 1962/1968, 1964/1970), and eventually to the founding of transpersonal psychology.

> *The fully developed (and very fortunate) human being, working under the best conditions tends to be motivated by values which transcend his self. They are not selfish anymore in the old sense of that term. Beauty is not within one's skin nor is justice or order. One can hardly class these desires as selfish in the sense that my desire for food might be. My satisfaction with achieving or allowing justice is not within my own skin; it does not lie along my arteries. It is equally outside and inside; therefore it has transcended the geographical limitations of the self.*
>
> (Maslow, 1969 p4).

Initially Maslow perceived these motivations as spiritual and therefore did not add them to his hierarchy of biologically rooted motivational needs. We are the products of evolution, and whatever characterizes the whole human species must be biological in nature. Only a percentage of human beings are motivated at this level, so he coined the terms 'metaneeds' and 'metamotivation', as if they were somehow beyond what could be defined as characteristic of the whole of the human species.

Thus self-actualization was still at the top of his hierarchy of universal, biologically rooted, motivating human needs. This meant that when Maslow wrote of self-actualizers, sometimes he meant those who are still pursuing further aspects of self-fulfilment and sometimes he meant those who are pursuing B-values i.e. metamotivated people (Maslow, 1962/1968).

Eventually this overlap was resolved when he finally conceded that these spiritual motivations are also part of our biological nature as members of the human species (Maslow, 1967). His friend and colleague Anthony Sutich wrote:

> *He told me that he had just completed writing a paper that was, in his own words, '....The culmination of 30 years of work in the field of psychology.'.... Maslow's manuscript arrived in June 1967.*

The title, 'A theory of metamotivation: The biological rooting of the value-life'....Was rather long and in conversation we referred to it as the 'metamotivation paper'.

(Sutich, 1976 p11).

The pursuit of what he had called 'metaneeds' could now be added to his hierarchy as a sixth level because it satisfied the criterion of being biologically rooted in our species just like the other five needs. Writing in his 'metamotivation paper' (these extracts taken from its reprint as Chapter 23 in *The Farther Reaches of Human Nature*, Maslow, 1976), Maslow said that 'These metaneeds, though having certain special characteristics which differentiate them from basic needs, are yet in the same realm of discourse and of research as, for instance, the need for vitamin C or for calcium' (p309). Basic needs and metaneeds were viewed '...in the same continuum, in the same realm of discourse... they are all biologically desirable, and all foster biological success' (pp311-312).

Although Maslow felt that intrinsic values are not '...fully evident or actualized (made real and functionally existing) in most people', he also wrote that the full definition of the person or of human nature must include them: '...they are not excluded as potentials in any human being born into the world' (p305), 'the so-called spiritual life is clearly rooted in the biological nature of the species' (p315).

These quotes demonstrate that Maslow finally considered the Hierarchy to include the so-called 'metaneeds', the need to pursue intrinsic values that transcend self-interest, as a sixth distinct level beyond the need to self-actualize. Yet so much of the literature on the subject overlooks this addition. All five preceding levels involve the individual's self-interest, including self-actualization, which is about achieving one's own full potential. It is at the sixth level that one is motivated by values that can be called 'ego-transcendent'. The two motivations that Maslow left unassigned in his seminal 1943 paper can also now be place at level six: the desire to know, and aesthetics, are to do with knowledge and truth, beauty and harmony, all of which are intrinsic values.

The metamotivation paper was published in the *Journal of Humanistic Psychology* (1967). This was a fledgling branch of psychology in the States and had not yet found its way into psychology on this side of the Atlantic, dominated as it was by psychoanalysis and behavioural psychology. It is unlikely to have been read over here by more than a handful of humanistic psychology pioneers. In January 1968 Maslow had his first serious heart attack and he died in June 1970 (Sutich, 1976 pp15/18). He therefore had little chance to consolidate his new perception of the Hierarchy, and he never actually spelled out in print the new list of motivational needs.

Values arising from religious beliefs are now addressed within transpersonal psychology, but at that time this embryonic branch of the profession had not yet been defined or even named, for it emerged with the first issue of the *Journal of Transpersonal Psychology* in 1969. Yet within transpersonal psychology today there does not seem to be an acknowledgement of these ego-transcendent motivations being separate from the ego-centred need to self-actualize.

It is a matter for regret that Maslow's insight concerning the addition of this level has gone almost unnoticed, especially as he described it as '...the culmination of 30 years of work in the field of psychology' (Sutich, 1976 p11). Had he lived longer I feel sure he would have built upon his new integrated theory of motivation embracing the physiological, emotional, social and spiritual aspects of human nature, together with its practical applications to the workplace and to society in general.

References

Maslow, A.H. (1943). A Theory of Human Motivation. *Psychological Review,* 50, 370-396. Reprinted as chapter 2 in *Motivation and Personality* (3rd edn), 1987.

Maslow, A.H. (1987). *Motivation and Personality* (3rd edn). New York: Harper & Row. (Original work published 1954.)

Maslow, A.H. (1968). *Toward a Psychology of Being* (2nd edn). New York: Van Nostrand. (Original work published 1962)

Maslow, A.H. (1970). *Religions, Values and Peak-experiences.* New York: Viking Press. (Original work published 1964)

Maslow, A.H. (1967). A theory of metamotivation. *Journal of Humanistic Psychology*, 7, 93-127. Reprinted as chapter 23 in *The Farther Reaches of Human Nature*, 1971.

Maslow, A.H. (1969). The farther reaches of human nature. *Journal of Transpersonal Psychology*, 1(1), 1-9.

Maslow, A.H. (1971). *The Farther Reaches of Human Nature*. New York: Viking Press.

Maslow, A.H. (1998). *Maslow On Management*. (D.C.Stephens & G.Heil, Eds.). New York: Wiley.

Sutich, A. (1976). The emergence of the transpersonal orientation: a personal account. *Journal of Transpersonal Psychology*, 8(1), 5-19.

FURTHER READING

For understanding personality, attitudes, reactions and behaviour:

Eric Berne, 1964. *Games People Play*. Penguin. An introduction to Transactional Analysis and a sometimes amusing catalogue of habitual patterns of response.

Daniel Goleman, 1995, UK 1996. *Emotional Intelligence*. Bloomsbury. In depth approach to understanding emotional responses and how to improve them.

Ian Gordon-Brown with Barbara Somers (ed. Hazel Marshall), 2008. *The Raincloud of Knowable Things*. Archive Publishing, Shaftesbury, Dorset, England. The complete original workshops of the Centre for Transpersonal Psychology, London. The sections on theory are comprehensive and informative. The exercises should be undertaken only with the guidance of a counsellor or psychotherapist who is qualified in transpersonal psychology.

Stanley Milgram, 1974. *Obedience to Authority*. Harper. An experiment which revealed the conflict between obedience to authority and compassion for victims.

Isabel Briggs Myers & Peter B. Myers, 1980. *Gifts Differing*. Consulting Psychologists Press. Analysis of different personality types and how to discover your own. Based on an extension of Carl Jung's theory of Four Functions, namely sensation, feeling, thinking and intuition.

Biographies

Edward Hoffman, 1988. *The Right to be Human*. Tarcher, USA. A comprehensive biography of Abraham Maslow.

C.G.Jung, 1963. *Memories, Dreams, Reflections* (English translation by Richard and Clara Winton). Autobiography of the psychiatrist Carl Jung. He gained self-understanding by interpreting his own dreams.

REFERENCES

Bible. King James version.

Penguin Encyclopedia, 2006, (ed. David Crystal). Revised third edition. London: Penguin Books.

Benson, Herbert with Miriam Z. Klipper, 1977. *The Relaxation Response*. London: Collins Fount Paperbacks. First published 1975, New York: William Morrow and Company.

Berne, Eric, 1968. *Games People Play*. Middlesex, England: Penguin Books. First published 1964, USA.

Enever, Ted, 1994. *Britain's Best Kept Secret: Ultra's Base at Bletchley Park*. Stroud, Gloucestershire, England: Sutton Publishing.

Gibson, Stephen, 2015. Rhetoric and Resistance. *The Psychologist, vol.28, no.8, August 2015, 648-651*. British Psychological Society.

Gordon-Brown, Ian, with Barbara Somers, 2008, (ed. Hazel Marshall). *The Raincloud of Knowable Things*. Archive Publishing, Shaftesbury, Dorset, England.

Grof, Stanislav, 1980. *LSD Psychotherapy*. Pomona, California: Hunter House.

Grof, Stanislav, 1985. *Beyond the Brain*. State University of New York Press.

Grof, Stanislav, 1988. *The Adventure of Self-Discovery*. State University of New York Press.

Grof, Stanislav & Christina Grof (eds.), 1989. *Spiritual Emergency*. Los Angeles, USA. Tarcher.

Guest, H, 1989. The origins of transpersonal psychology. *British Journal of Psychotherapy, vol.6, 62-69*.

Guest, H, 1990. Sequential Analysis: monitoring counselling sessions via skin resistance. *Counselling Psychology Quarterly, vol.3, no.1, 85-91.*

Guest, Hazel, 1995. Rising from the ashes: recovery from physical trauma. *British Journal of Guidance and Counselling, vol.23, no.1, 115-126.*

Guest, Hazel Skelsey, 2014. Maslow's Hierarchy of Needs: the Sixth Level. *The Psychologist, vol.27, no.12, December 2014, 982-983.* British Psychological Society.

Guest, Hazel & Ian Marshall, 1997. The Scale of responses: emotions and mood in context. *International Journal of Psychotherapy, vol.2, no.2, 149-169.*

Jacobi, Jolande, 1968 (transl. Ralph Manheim). *The Psychology of C.G. Jung.* Seventh edition. England: Routledge & Kegan Paul. First published in England 1942 by RKP.

Janov, Arthur, 1973. *The Primal Scream.* Abacus edition. London: Sphere Books.

Jung, C.G, 1959. *The Collected Works.* Edited by Sir Herbert Read, Michael Fordham and Gerhard Adler, and translated into English by R.F.C.Hull. Routledge & Kegan Paul.

Maslow, Abraham H, 1943. A theory of human motivation. *Psychology Review, vol.50, 370-396.* Reprinted as chapter 2 in his book *Motivation and Personality* and in many other books and journals.

Maslow, Abraham H, 1967. A theory of metamotivation: the biological rooting of the value life. *Journal of Humanistic Psychology, vol.67, 93-127.* Reprinted as chapter 23 in his book *The Farther Reaches of Human Nature.*

Maslow, Abraham H, 1968 (2nd edn.). *Towards a Psychology of Being.* New York: D.Van Nostrand. Original work published in 1962.

Maslow, Abraham H, 1970. *Religions, Values and Peak Experiences.* New York: Viking Press. Original work published in 1964 by Kappa

Delta Pi.

Maslow, Abraham H, 1976. *The Farther Reaches of Human Nature*. Middlesex, England: Penguin Books. Original work published in 1971 in the USA by Viking Press.

Maslow, Abraham H, 1987. *Motivation and Personality* (3rd edn.). New York: Harper & Row. Original work published in 1954.

Maslow, Abraham H, 1998, edited by D. C. Stephens & G. Heil, *Maslow On Management*. New York: Wiley.

Marx, Karl, 1844, *A Contribution to the Critique of Hegel's Philosophy of Right*.

Milgram, Stanley, 1975. *Obedience to Authority*. New York: Harper & Row.

Minett, Gunnel, 1994. *Breath & Spirit – Rebirthing as a Healing Technique*. London: Aquarian Press.

Norberg-Hodge, Helena, 1992. *Ancient Futures: Learning from Ladakh*. London: Rider. First published 1991 in the USA by Sierra Club Books.

Pope, Alexander, 1711. *An Essay on Criticism*.

Rowan, J, 1993. *The Transpersonal: Psychotherapy and Counselling*. London: Routledge.

Suzuki, D.T, 1949, (ed. Christmas Humphreys). *An Introduction to Zen Buddhism*. May 1969 edition. London: Rider.

Wilber, Ken, 1980. *The Atman Project*. Wheaton, Illinois, USA: The Theosophical Publishing House.

Wilber, Ken, 2000. *Integral Psychology*. Boston: Shambhala.

NOTES

Preface

1. Abraham Maslow (1908-1970) was born in Manhattan, New York. He studied psychology at the University of Wisconsin in Madison, and did his doctoral research on the behaviour of monkeys. In 1937 he became psychology tutor at Brooklyn College, New York City. In 1943 his paper 'A Theory of Human Motivation' containing his famous Hierarchy of Needs, was published. It became known worldwide and acquired its now-familiar representation in the form of a triangle. In 1951 he was appointed head of psychology at Brandeis University, Boston, Massachusetts. In 1962 he was elected President of the American Psychological Association.

The Hierarchy of Needs became influential for its applications to the world of management, particularly for improving the motivation of workers in factories and businesses. He spent the summer of 1962 with the engineering firm Non-Linear Systems in Del Mar, California, observing the application of his ideas in practice, and the notes he made there were eventually published (*Maslow on Management*, published by Wiley, 1998 is an edited edition).

His interest in what constitutes a healthy society led him to found the 'Eupsychian Network' which in 1962 became the Association for Humanistic Psychology. It publishes the Journal of Humanistic Psychology. He also became interested in peak-experiences which led him to join with other colleagues in founding the Journal of Transpersonal Psychology, the first issue of which appeared in 1969.

In 1967 he added a sixth level to the Hierarchy of Needs, namely *Intrinsic Values*. That same year he had a heart attack followed by a general deterioration in health, and died in June 1970.

2. Maslow, 1943,1987.

3. Maslow, 1967.

4. Dr Ian N. Marshall (1931-2012) read mathematics at Oxford University followed by taking a degree in psychology and philosophy.

After that he took a medical degree at the University of London, and subsequently practised as a Jungian psychiatrist and psychotherapist in London. He was the author of several academic papers, and with his wife Danah Zohar co-authored the books *The Quantum Self, The Quantum Society, Spiritual Intelligence, Spiritual Capital*, and *Who's Afraid of Schrodinger's Cat?*. Having moved to Oxford they both taught at Oxford Brookes University and lectured worldwide.

5. Guest, 1990.

6. Guest & Marshall, 1997.

7. Maslow, 1998.

Part 1: Needs Must

Chapter 2 The Motivation Hierarchy

1. See the Preface, note 2.

2. See the Preface, note 1.

3. See the Preface, note 3.

Chapter 9 Intrinsic Values

1. This level of the Hierarchy has been known by a variety of names. In the 1970's at the pioneering Centre for Transpersonal Psychology in London it was referred to as Self-Realization.

When employed as a mathematics lecturer at City University, London, I called this level 'Ego-Transcendence' in the course on transpersonal psychology which I designed and ran from 1979 to the mid-1980's as a General Studies option for engineering, maths and science students. This was the first ever course on transpersonal psychology to be an essential part of a degree in any British university.

Ken Wilber refers to this level of the Hierarchy as 'transcendence' or 'self-transcendence' (table 4 in Wilber 1980 and chart 7 in Wilber 2000).

Here Maslow's own term 'intrinsic values' is being used for the sake of historical accuracy. In the Appendix will be found an explanation of how he finally came to acknowledge this level as an essential part of his Hierarchy of biologically-rooted motivating needs.

2. 'We share the need for food with all living things, the need for love with (perhaps) the higher apes, the need for self-actualization with nobody.' (quoted in the Appendix). Page 57 in Maslow, 1987.

Chapter 10 Pre-potency
1. The triangular representation for the Hierarchy was introduced by someone unknown. Maslow never actually used this pictorial form and instead always just named the needs in order, starting with the physiological needs (he did not include survival).
2. Maslow, 1968.

Chapter 11 Childhood
1. Berne, 1968.
2. Guest, 1995.

Chapter 12 Deficiency
1. See the chapter on Pre-potency.

Chapter 14 Curiosity
1. A grandmother clock is similar to a grandfather clock except that the pendulum and the case in which it is housed are shorter. A complete swing back and forth takes one second instead of two.
2. See the Preface, note 2.

Chapter 15 The Urge to Fit In
1. See chapter on Pre-potency.

Chapter 16 Guilt and Shame
1. Enever, 1994. Also: The film *The Imitation Game* starring Benedict Cumberbatch as Alan Turing.

Chapter 18 Power and Love
1. The psychiatrist Carl Jung (1875-1961) developed the theory of archetypes.
2. See the chapters on Childhood and Deficiency.
3. Jung, 1959. *Volume9, Part 1: The Archetypes and the Collective Unconscious.*
4. See the chapter on Deficiency.
5. Lord Acton (1834-1902) English historian and moralist, in a letter to Bishop Mandell Creighton.
6. Milgram, 1975.
7. See also example 14 in chapter 41.

8. John 15:13.

Chapter 19 The Profit Motive

1. An example can be found in Norberg-Hodge, 1992.

2. See the Appendix for an account of how he came to change his mind
.

Chapter 20 Religion

1. From Marx, (1844).

2. Richard Dawkins, zoologist. 'He remains a controversial media figure, known as much for his aggressive atheism as for his scientific views on evolution.' (Penguin Encyclopedia, 2006)

Chapter 22 Revenge

1. From the laws of justice as laid down in Exodus 21:24 and Deuteronomy 19:21.

2. See chapter 1.

3. In Romans 12:19 Paul refers to Deuteronomy 32:35.

4. Matthew 5:44.

Chapter 23 The Shadow

1. Carl Jung wrote extensively about the Shadow in *The Collected Works*, 1959.

For a brief introduction to the Shadow see pages 109-114 in Jacobi, 1968.

2. Books by the psychiatrist Stanislav Grof link his earlier research into LSD (Grof, 1980) with the effects of the birth trauma and what he has termed 'spiritual emergencies' (Grof & Grof, 1989). This work relates to -6:Depersonalization on the Scale of Responses (chapter 34 in Part 2).

Chapter 25 Know Thyself

1. Penguin Encyclopedia, 2006.

Part 2: Step by Step

Chapter 26 How Did That Happen?

1. See the Preface, note 4.

2. See the Preface, note 5.

3. See the Preface, note 6.

Chapter 31   Retreat and Participation

1. 'Lie detectors' do not accurately detect lies. Instead they detect reactions in the psyche which may, or may not, be due to the attempt to lie.

For an introduction to the use of galvanic skin resistance meters in psychotherapy see Guest, 1990.

2. See chapter 39 for -2:Attack contained within +3:Participation.

Chapter 34   Depersonalization and Transpersonalization

1. Maslow introduced the term 'peak experiences' for these phenomena. See Maslow, 1970.

2. See the chapters in Part 1 on Childhood and Deficiency.

3. See the Preface, note 5. The misleading correlation of low/high skin resistance with stress/relaxation was based upon research into the practice of Transcendental Meditation which is of the concentrative type. (Chapter 37, 'One Step at a Time', note 4).

Research into insight meditation is problematical because it is impossible to predict if and when an insight will occur. The GSR correlates to a therapeutic insight can only be observed when a GSR meter is used to monitor counselling and psychotherapy sessions by someone trained in such techniques. See Guest, 1990.

4. Guest, 1990.

5. See pages 103-110 in Minett, 1994. Also Janov, 1973. For a more academic approach, Grof, 1988.

6. See the chapter on Childhood in Part 1.

7. For an explanation of the inner self and transpersonal concepts see Guest, 1989 and Rowan, 1993.

8. Grof, 1980. Also several sections in Grof 1985 and 1988.

Chapter 36   Personal Norm

1. For an introduction to the theory of subpersonalities and how to discover them, see: Gordon-Brown and Somers, 2008. The exercises it contains should be undertaken only with supervision by a counsellor or psychotherapist qualified to run workshops in transpersonal psychology.

Chapter 37   One Step at a Time

1. D.T.Suzuki, 1949, page 95.

2. Containment is the subject of chapter 39.

3. For vulnerability see the chapters on Childhood and Deficiency in

Part 1. Also see Guest, 1995.

4. Transcendental Meditation was popularised in the West in the late 1960's by the Maharishi Mahesh Yogi and the Beatles. It involves concentration on a mantra. An indication of the differences between concentrative and insight meditations can be found in the chapter on Depersonalization and Transpersonalization.

Chapter 40 Subpersonalities
1. See chapter 36, note 1.

Chapter 41 Examples for Analysis
1. See chapter 18 note 6.
2. Adapted from the account given in Gibson, 2015.

Chapter 42 Analyses
1. See notes 1 and 2 for chapter 41.
2. Radicalisation in prisons was discussed in relation to the Motivation Hierarchy in the chapter on Deficiency in Part 1.
3. For the formation of unconscious programmes see the chapters in Part 1 on Childhood and Deficiency.

Chapter 43 Knowledge and Wisdom
1. Pope, 1711.
2. For motivation and unconscious programmes, see Part 1.

Part 3: Conclusion

Chapter 44 Continuum
1. Benson, 1977.
2. Dian Fossey, 1932-1985, primatologist, pioneered the study of mountain gorillas in Rwanda. Her 1983 book 'Gorillas in the Mist' was made into a film in 1988.
3. The naturalist Sir David Attenborough is famous for his documentaries on the natural world for the BBC.

INDEX